High School

RICH

101 HOT TIPS TO SUCCESS

BY WENDY PERKINS

ISBN: 1463568150
ISBN-13: 9781463568153

Printed in the USA

A gift for

_____

From

_____

Dedication

*T*his book is dedicated to all the parents who want their kids to mature into law-abiding, self-sufficient, and financially secure individuals (basically so they can leave the nest and only come back to visit!).

We are all great individuals. Discover your inner greatness, embrace it, and grow into a self-reliant and self-sufficient being on the road to success. *This book is your manual.*

Acknowledgments

I wish to express my sincerest appreciation to my kids, Chelsea, and Cameron, for their constant encouragement and support.

To my dad, Moses Brown Sr., in loving memory, thank you for teaching me, not to be afraid of a challenge.

To my mom, Ethel Brown, for your unwavering faith in me.

To Ellen Burton for your unlimited wholehearted help on this project.

To Moultrie for your infusion of energy to get this book done.

To Robert Jr., for your many thought-provoking conversations.

To Roy and Genora Morgan for encouraging me to live my dream.

To all my additional family and friends that supported me, thank you.

Preface

As a native Floridian, I have enjoyed working in the field of mortgage lending, real estate, investments, and landownership. With the ability to maintain a flexible schedule, I was able to devote many hours of my time to young adults, which was a prequel to becoming the author of *High School Rich: 101 Hot Tips to Success.*

I have gathered much insight from my many years of mentoring, counseling, and encouraging young adults. Realizing that all kids could benefit from my knowledge, I decided to put the information into book form to assist more young people, from adolescence to adulthood, in pursuing financial and entrepreneurial independence.

I was fortunate to develop an entrepreneurial mind at an early age. My dad was self-employed for over forty years and managed to support a family of eight people and a dog without any of us ever experiencing the feeling of want. Some of the other families we knew were struggling to make ends meet; meanwhile, we wore the latest styles, had new cars, and went on trips to my grandparents' homes.

I realized that owning your own business gave you a lot of freedom with your time and money. Some weeks, our family required additional funds, and that meant my dad had to work a little harder that week, but he always managed to make the money we needed. If he had worked on a nine-to-five schedule, our family would have felt the stress of money problems. When you work on a job and get paid by the hour, you can only work so many hours in a day. If you need extra that week, you just can't work extra hours; you must get approval and hope that the extra hours are needed by the company. Who wants to have to depend on so many factors to fall just right in order to make a little extra money?

I always enjoyed the way we could take a trip and not have to worry about my mom and dad losing their jobs. I knew then that was the type of job I wanted to do. I wanted to have that freedom to experience life without the hassle of corporate constraints.

Even though we were not rich, we never lacked for anything. We never knew that based on some statistics, we were poor. Go figure. In this instance, what I did not know did not hurt me. My parents were positive-thinking people. Positive-thinking and positive reinforcement can stir a child toward positive outcomes.

My mom and dad grew up in the South and did not have all the advantages that others were afforded. That never hindered my parents' thinking; neither did it stop them from requiring all of us to become productive, law–abiding, self-sufficient, and educated individuals. All of my siblings have created their own empires—some through conventional ways and some through entrepreneurial actions. It all depends on what fits the lifestyle you want to have and your empire and whatever that means to you.

As I moved on to my adult life, I continued to be focused and unwavering in my desire to create my empire. Having my own empire entailed the ability to come and go as I pleased. I did not want to be time restricted. I did not want to have to report to a supervisor and not be able to take a day off without making up some illness. I wanted the opposite of all of these things; I just did not know how to get that, so I got a job. I worked and saved my money and purchased my first condo. The bank held the first mortgage, and the seller held the second mortgage. I paid off the second mortgage as soon as I could and was on my way to creating my individual empire.

Sharing this information is a way of giving back to society and a vehicle for providing youth with a positive way to become productive members of society, with the fulfillment that can be achieved from being financially independent.

Knowledge is power, and time brings on wisdom. I hope you get as much knowledge from this book and gain as much wisdom as I did in creating my individual empire.

This book was designed to equip you with the tools to create your own individual empire. If you apply these tools, you will make money. The amount of money you make is totally up to you.

Visit me at
www.HighSchoolRich.com

Contents

Acknowledgments   *vii*
Preface   *ix*

Part One: Rich in Knowledge   1
Win the Oscar!   *3*
Dream Big   *5*
Bust It Loose   *9*
Your Most Powerful Weapon   *13*
The Best and Brightest   *15*
High School Divided   *17*

Part Two: Rich in Business   95
Entrepreneurs   *99*
Bankable facts   *107*
Credit Credit Credit   *109*
The entrepreneur with us   *113*
Sweat equity   *119*

Part Three: Rich in Friendship   131
Value your friends   *133*
Who's on your team   *135*
Haters   *137*
Know your worth   *141*
Have a mentor   *145*

Part Four: Rich in Thoughts   151
Law and order   *153*
Don't climb the mountain   *157*
Live your dreams   *159*
101 hot tips   *165*

Part Five: Rich in Jobs   179
Show me the money   *181*
Dog walking   *183*
Lawn service   *189*
Other businesses   *191*

Appendix: Journal   193

Part One

Rich in Knowledge

Win the Oscar!

Think of your life as a movie. You are the writer, director, producer, and star. You choose your costars and extras. Whether the movie is a smash or a flop is in your hands.

Every thought you have and every decision you make will write the script for the movie of your life. Develop your mind early with as much information as possible. The more information you have, the better the decisions you will make. Good decisions create great writing, which ultimately produces a hit movie.

Along the way, you may have to rewrite parts of the script. Don't worry; hiccups happen sometimes. Rewrite the script, get back on course, and keep it moving. Struggle builds character and makes you a wiser person. The more wisdom you gain, the more knowledge you will desire.

Knowledge is power. You should never exhaust your desire to learn and understand new things. Do not be afraid to implement the things you have learned on a daily basis within your life movie.

As you read, understand, and implement the suggestions in this book, you will begin your journey toward making a smash-hit movie.

Dream Big

The future is yours for the taking. Success is within the reach of every individual. Dream big, and envision yourself at the top. Every empire starts with a dream. Along with dreams, we have hopes—hence the phrase "hopes and dreams." We would be lost if we had no hope. Without hope, reality cannot be manifested. Seek upward mobility; do not settle for the status quo.

Some think most things are out of their reach and only attainable for others. That type of thinking will nail you to the floor and not allow you to move forward. Do you want to wish for success or have success?

Put your thoughts into action, and watch the world open up to you. It does not matter what part of the world you are from or what part of the city you grew up in. What does matter is the size of your dream, the depth of your passion and commitment, and your willingness to sacrifice to obtain your dream. The bigger the dream, the bigger the win.

List your dreams:

1) _____

2) _____

3) _____

4) _____

Bust It Loose

We all have an entrepreneurial spirit within us; some develop theirs, and others don't. Some of the richest individuals in the world are entrepreneurs. The only difference between those individuals and you is the size of the dream and the initiative to act upon the dream.

Walt Disney

Walt Disney began his dream in the early 1900s. Animation was unheard of at that time, but that did not stop Walt Disney from chasing his dream. Despite early failures, including losing the rights to his first animated character (Waldo the Rabbit), and filing for bankruptcy, he eventually created one of the greatest multidisciplinary entertainment companies in history. He was focused, determined, and believed in his dream. There are now Disneyland's and Disney Worlds in the United States, Mexico, Canada, Japan, Korea, and Australia.

Bill Gates, Microsoft

His vision was that someday, everyone would have a personal computer on his or her desk. In the 1970s, that seemed like science fiction, but it turns out his vision led to one of the greatest transformative events in the history of business.

Ray Kroc, McDonald's

He was almost fifty years old when he saw the McDonald's brothers' shiny hamburger stand in Southern California. Kroc created assembly-line food, along with the largest chain of restaurants in the world (serving more than fifty million people daily). He also invented franchising.

Henry Ford, Ford Motor Company

Like many entrepreneurs, Henry Ford saw big failure before he found big success. His first two car companies went out of business. He kept at it and went on to invent the assembly line, which made cars in a more cost-effective way. He also created the five-dollar-a-day wage so that his own employees could afford to buy his car, and, in the process, Ford essentially helped create the American middle class, along with revolutionizing personal transportation.

All of these individuals were born; learned to crawl, walk, and talk; went to school; and played in their yards. These people are no different from you or me. Believe in yourself, and dream big. When you couple these with action and commitment, you will be on your way to building your own empire as an entrepreneur.

"All our dreams can come true, if we have the courage to pursue them" —Walt Disney

---

*H*ey, Jimmy, check your e-mail, jump in the car, stop for gas, cash your check, grab a burger and Coke, and shop for a discount Mickey Mouse T-shirt before coming home.

How many entrepreneurs did it take to create this sentence?

Answer: 8

Can you list the eight entrepreneurs?

1.

2.

3.

4.

5.

6.

7.

8.

1. Bill Gates, Microsoft; 2. Henry Ford, Ford Motor Company; 3. John D. Rockefeller, Standard Oil; 4. Amadeo P. Giannini, Bank of America; 5. Ray Kroc, McDonald's; 6. Asa Candler, Coca-Cola; 7. Walt Disney, Disney; 8.Sam Walton, Wal-Mart.

Entrepreneur tip:

Education is the key that unlocks the

door to success

Your Most Powerful Weapon

Education is the most powerful weapon,
which you can use to change the world.

—Nelson Mandela

Educate yourself, become well informed, and simply learn, learn, and learn. The more you learn about any situation, the more you will feel in control of things. The more you educate yourself and the more you build your knowledge of the things around you, the more you will realize that knowledge is powerful.

What you put in year head cannot be taken from you. Owning material things is great, but accumulating a plethora of knowledge is the ultimate success. Cars can be repossessed, houses foreclosed, and Blackberry's lost, but your knowledge is forever. Invest in the possession you are guaranteed to have the rest of your life. Knowledge is growth, and ignorance is chaos.

Youth is no excuse for allowing educational and entrepreneurial opportunities to pass you by. When you're young, you sometimes think or feel like you are invincible. You want to conquer the world, not just now but later, because you have all the time in the world to make all your dreams come true. That is not realistic thinking. Time is not endless, and every moment is precious. Do not waste valuable moments. Make every moment count. Enjoy your life, and make well-thought-out choices. Choose to be educated; learn and absorb as soon as possible.

Some individuals have natural talents in various things. So much emphasis is placed on their natural talents that education is neglected. What happens when your natural ability to play sports or music, create art, or do other nonacademic things does not work out the way you planned? Here's an example:

John is the high school athlete of the year and receives a full, four-year scholarship to attend ABC University. He spends all his time making the coach, teammates, and fans happy and does not take his education seriously. John gets drafted to the NFL and does not complete his education. He earns a lot of money and does not invest any of it, nor does he continue his education.

John gets injured and doesn't have a backup plan. If John had been educated, he would have known how to read the fine print in the contract that stated he was not entitled to any injury compensation. The next time we see John, he's broke and homeless, due to his lack of education and his inability to comprehend the details of his contract. You don't want to make the same mistake as John.

If you happen to excel at sports and want to use that as plan A, make sure to have a plan B and C. The average person will sometime have a plan B, but a successful person always has a plan B and even a plan C. *Education* is the best plan to have. It is vital to your success. Being educated allows you to have *options.*

No matter what you want to do in life, you need to have a plan; research your plan, and execute your plan. Read good materials and good books to develop your life plan, and the world will open up to you.

The Best and Brightest

If you rely on your information source to be within your circle, you will only be as smart as the brightest person in the group. If you have Albert Einstein, Ludwig Wittgenstein, or Sir Isaac Newton in your circle, it may be okay to rely on the brightest in your circle. I can say with great certainty that these individuals are not in your circle.

Surround yourself with knowledgeable and wise individuals, but don't rely on others as your only information source. Utilize the Internet and your local libraries as much as possible. The more you read, the more you are prepared for life. Read books. Read from the Internet. Read from all available sources.

Some of us will not be able to physically see the world. But through the resources of the Internet and our libraries, the world is available to everyone. If you want to know how families live on the other side of the world, simply get a library card and visit your library, where you can read a book and enjoy the use of the Internet. You can learn about anything in the world as if you were there.

The world is at your fingertips through books and the Internet. Read to increase your vocabulary. Read to know the world around you. Read to learn about any subject. Read to prepare yourself for life.

Journal Your Thoughts

High School Divided

I *went to high school with a lot of motivated and intelligent kids.* We were all from the same neighborhood and similar backgrounds. Everyone had the same chance at a *productive life.*

There came a time when we all began to make choices that would affect our lives. At that time, none of us knew or took the time to understand the consequences of our decisions. We did not realize then that the choices we were making in high school would determine where we would be in life *thirty years later.*

Life has changed for a lot of the kids in my class. Some made the decision to have unprotected sex and now have diseases that modern medicine cannot cure. Some made the decision to hang out with kids their parents did not approve of. Those kids now have criminal records or are addicted to drugs. Others decided to play by the rules and make better choices. Those kids are now adults with their own restaurants, clothing stores, mortgage companies, and so on.

The point to this story is that all of your choices follow you throughout your life. Let your choices be positive and well thought out. Because what you choose to do today will contribute to the outcome of tomorrow. All your decisions and choices determine the quality of life you will experience. Begin early to make the right decisions.

Do not waste any of your life. Life is precious and special; it is a gift. Create your empire with good decisions coupled with excellent choices. Develop this quality early in life by developing your mind.

At your twenty-year reunion, what will be your outcome?

Entrepreneur tip:

Closed mouths don't get fed.

(Old saying)

*O*pen your mouth and ask for what you want in life and out of your life. Don't be afraid to verbalize your needs, wants and desires in business and in your personal life. The alternative to asking for what you want is to walk around hoping someone will figure it out. No one can read your mind. Be direct and learn to properly communicate your thoughts. The best way to get what you want is to simply ask for it.

"If you don't go after what you want, you'll never have it. If you don't ask, the answer is always no. If you don't step forward, you're always in the same place." —Nora Roberts

---

The Mind Is a Muscle

Developing *your mind early is as important to the success of your empire as exercising is to the well-being of your body.* The *mind* is a muscle. That muscle requires the same attention that you would give to your biceps or triceps. If you want to stay in shape and develop those muscles, you must consistently do various exercises. The brain is the physical part of the mind, and the mind is the actual working part of the brain.

The mind is constantly learning and absorbing information; however, you need to put the mind to work by practicing some simple exercises that will enhance it. For example, do not use a calculator when figuring simple math problems; use your mind. When traveling with your parents to a new location, use a map and not the GPS to direct you to your destination.

These simple exercises, along with a healthy diet, regular physical exercise, good stress management, healthy sleep habits, and refraining from smoking, will help your mind to become more alert and allow it to function at its maximum level.

Reading, learning, and applying what you've learned is the *gateway to success.* Most wealthy people have a library in their homes. The library is filled with books that open up a wealth of knowledge. A person who reads books, studies, and applies the knowledge gained becomes increasingly proficient in developing his or her mind. To build a successful life, you must have a library of books. A library is a source for lifelong learning. Learning is a lifelong adventure.

As you continue to evolve, you must read as much as possible to improve the way you learn. Remember, your earning ability is in direct proportion to your learning ability. The more you learn, the more you will earn.

Sit in the front of the class and listen to your instructors. Be attentive and active in class. Train your mind to comprehend and apply. Develop your mind early in your life, and when you're ready to create your business, you will be better prepared.

This book is designed to equip you with the tools to create your own individual empire. If you apply these tools, you will make money. The amount of money you make is totally up to you.

Think Success

Imagination is everything. It is the preview
of life's coming attractions.

—Albert Einstein (Winner, Nobel Prize in Physics)

Use your imagination to visualize your success.
Creative visualization is the use of your imagination to create
success in all areas of your life. *Visualize success*; this is one of
the easiest things you can do to expand your success. If you can
visualize and see yourself successful, the battle is won. If you can
conceive it and *perceive it*, you can *achieve it*. Visualization is the *key*
to success.

Your mind uses visualization all the time, both consciously
and unconsciously. We must train ourselves to exercise our
imagination to direct our thoughts in a positive direction. When
we are unsuccessful, most times, it is a direct result of negative
visualization.

If you're seeking employment and you visualize yourself in
the position, you will project that positive result into reality.
When you visualize failing the interview process and not getting
the job, that negative result that you have embedded in your
thought process will occur and you will not get that job. When
visualizing, use your imagination. Imagine yourself getting the

job; becoming successful, happy, and healthy; and living all your dreams. Your journey in life will often reflect what you envision.

All of us have an imagination. This quality is only valuable when we *unlock the trait*. Here's how to unlock that trait and get your imagination flowing:

- Close your eyes, and envision what you want. If it's a new car, envision the make, model, and color of the car. Imagine yourself driving down the highway with the top down and the wind blowing in your face.
- Imagine yourself succeeding at everything you set your mind to do. If it's getting a job, envision yourself waking up early for the interview, making a great impression on the interviewer, and getting that job.
- Get visualization helpers. Some people prefer to have inspirational pictures—for example, pictures that have inspirational quotes at the bottom. Utilize vision boards and goal books where you can paste or draw pictures that symbolize what you're trying to achieve.
- Imagine yourself when you have accomplished your task successfully, the happiness and joy that comes with that.
- Visualize yourself as empowered, resilient, and confident. These thoughts will flow over into everything that you do. Nothing will be too big to conquer. Follow these steps consistently. Repetition helps to maintain and reinforce positive thoughts, which lead to contentment, confidence, and empowerment.

Couple positive visualization with positive thinking, and success will follow. Positive thinking leads to inner peace, good health, happiness, and positive results. Positive thinking is a mental attitude that admits certain thoughts, words, and images into the mind.

No matter what the circumstances are in your life or what the state of the economy, positive thinking can have a *positive effect*. In order for positive thinking to yield positive results, you need to develop a positive attitude. To do this, you must allow positive thoughts to penetrate your psyche. Incorporate the following into your everyday living:

- Visualize positive results.
- Use positive words and phrases like *I can*; *it can be done*; and *it's possible.*
- Read inspirational books.
- Ignore negative thoughts.
- Associate with positive people.
- Use the law of attraction.
- Positive attracts positive.
- Develop positive habits.

Positive thinking is contagious. People around you will pick up on the positive vibrations that you are emitting. We all have friends who are pessimists. Some people are just born that way. We tend to reflect our surroundings, so make a *conscious effort* to surround yourself with positive, progressive, and optimistic individuals.

Success is not something that reveals itself to an elite few. Anyone at any time can be successful. Remember, our minds believe what we tell them. When we continue to tell ourselves something, good or bad, positive or negative, our brain registers it.

Step-by-step our brain will learn to accept all that we give it and will give us back what we put in. If positive and good in equals positive and good out, then negative and bad in must equal negative and bad out. Feed your brain with positive thoughts, not *mind pollutants.* Use your imagination to visualize positive results and surround yourself with positive people, and you will be successful. You hold the power to achieve your success.

Your Turn

Complete the following: I can think success into everything I do by

_____

_____

_____

_____

I've Got the Power

The power you are required to have to become successful is willpower. *Willpower* is the ability to overcome procrastination and laziness. It is the ability to control or reject harmful impulses. It is the ability to make a decision and follow through to its successful conclusion with *perseverance*. Willpower is that inner power that we have that helps us to overcome the desire to indulge in unimportant, unhealthy, useless, and unnecessary habits, thoughts, and feelings.

Sometimes, even though you want to study, knowing how good it would be for your grades and how happy getting an A would make you feel, instead of proceeding to study, you watch TV. You are aware of the fact that you need to break the bad habit of watching TV instead of taking time to study. In order to make the proper decision, you must have willpower and *discipline*.

Train your mind to obey you. Strengthen your inner power and gain inner strength. Your muscles get stronger as you exercise them. The more you pump the barbells and use resistance, the more your muscles progress and get stronger. The same is true with strengthening your willpower and discipline. Inner strength is attained by overcoming inner resistance.

Here are a few exercises that you can do to train your mind to overcome procrastination, laziness, or lack of assertiveness.

1. If you come home and you have homework to do, resist the temptation to watch TV and do your homework later.

Do your homework as soon as you get home. Do not procrastinate.

2. When you arrive home and dishes are in the sink, don't take a nap; wash the dishes. Overcome the laziness.

3. Physical exercise is crucial to the well-being of your body. Even though we know we need to exercise, sometimes we'd rather not take the time to do it. Use your willpower to push through the desire not to do the exercise.

4. It is important to participate in class. Listen to the instructor. Do not sit there idle. Use your assertiveness to answer your instructor's questions.

These are just a few of the things you can do to increase your willpower and self-discipline. Think of a few more examples of ways to increase your inner strength, which will lead to having stronger willpower and discipline with which to build your foundation of success.

1) _____

2) _____

3) _____

The Foundation

The key to building success is creating a solid foundation. This entails an understanding of the following basic principles:

1. **Build associations**—Associations are the connections you create or establish between you and two or more people. You want to strive to build relationships with like-minded people. If you're looking to become an investor, then it would benefit you to acquaint and associate yourself with other investors. The fact is there are a lot of different types of investments; therefore, it would be wise to listen and absorb the wisdom of those around you when they speak about their different types of investments and financial dealings.

2. **Build healthy relationships**—A relationship is a significant connection or similarity between two or more individuals. The catch phrase "Birds of a feather flock together" is very apropos. It would be monotonous to have the same likes and dislikes with all of your friends, so it is important to have the same and yet at the same time different types of thinking. Respect each other's ideas and principles, providing there is no harm done to others. What you read, write, hear, and see has a huge influence on the person you will become. Keep in mind, Mom was always right when she would say, "Tell me who you hang around with and I'll tell who you are."

3. **Garbage in garbage out** (an old cliché)—This applies to the mind as well as the body. The phrase "You are what you eat" means the healthier the food, the healthier the body and

the clearer the mind. The better you're equipped to maintain good health, the more likely you'll keep a sound mind and functioning body. Good health creates a sound mind and increases your ability to create rational thinking while you build the basic foundations toward achieving your personal empire.

4. **Create beneficial behaviors and characteristics**.
   a. Trust your instincts. These are sometimes called "gut feelings." Be willing to take on challenges and calculated risks—notice I said *calculated* risks.
   b. Walk like a successful person. Have a swagger in your step. Walk with your head up…but not stuck up! Have and maintain good posture; stand firm. A person who is hunched over practically looking down most of the time does not project a positive image of himself or herself.
   c. Talk like a successful person. Always strive to continuously expand your vocabulary almost on a daily basis. Speak with authority and command attention when speaking, always of course, without being rude or obnoxious. Use correct enunciation. Read biographies of famous and successful people and emulate them; apply their experiences to your life dealings and principles (see suggested book list).
   d. Associate yourself with those who have already and continue to achieve success. Learn all you can from your own experiences and the experiences of others. Life experiences will teach you tremendous lessons. Remember, we learn from experiences and not all experiences are rewarding. Sometimes our experiences may seem like failures or we are not as successful as we would have hoped, but there is nothing wrong with that. We learn from those situations too, as you will learn when reading about the lives of other successful individuals, such as William Gates III, Warren Buffett, Jim Walton, and Michael Dell. Sometimes the worst failures are turned around into great successes. Use practical application. On-the-job training gives you hands-on experience.
   e. Dress for success and learn proper etiquette. A high percentage of first impressions are based on visual

assessments. The first seven seconds are crucial in evaluating an image of the person you are meeting or creating an image of yourself for the person meeting you. Dress to impress. Carefully assess the attire you choose to wear for that specific occasion. Determine the event, and choose your wardrobe accordingly. If you do not know the appropriate dress code for specific instances, ask those more knowledgeable than you for advice.

Guys, include a power tie (red) in your wardrobe. Girls, include a power suit (navy blue) in your wardrobe.

5. **Create a good first impression**
   a. The greeting and the handshake, along with eye contact, are as vitally important as the attire. A weak handshake projects weakness to the person you are greeting, thus creating a feeling of superiority on his or her part. I call it a "mullet or salmon handshake." Can you imagine shaking hands with a dead fish? Of course not. You want to keep the greeting on an equal level, meaning that neither you nor the person you're greeting has a feeling of superiority over the other. This, as in any business dealing, should be a *win-win* situation. This means that at a first encounter with someone, you both feel equal to each other.
   b. Now, within those first seconds, as I mentioned earlier, there comes an equally vital sign: *eye contact.* Look the person you are greeting for the first time directly in the eyes. Always have a warm and friendly smile. Listen to the person's name, or when you give your firm handshake (please, no vise grips either), ask for his or her name if he or she hasn't already given it to you. Always repeat the name back to the person. A name is the biggest identity marker a person owns. It's an important part of him or her. This little detail will help you in a matter of two or three seconds, in two distinct ways: 1) it shows the person you're greeting that you've made a personal connection with him or her; and 2) it creates a secondary memory jogger for you to remember his or her name.

Plan for the Future

Events that have not yet happened are called the future. Your future has the possibility to have a more positive outcome. You may change the outcome simply by changing your actions. Doing positive things and having positive thoughts will change the course of your future. What you do today will always affect the outcome of tomorrow.

Once you start school, the more you prepare for a class, the better the grade you will receive. The better the grades, the better the chance of receiving a scholarship to pay for a college education. That is called planning for the future. You want to do this in every aspect of life. On a job, your opportunity for advancement becomes more likely if you prepare yourself properly for the job. Planning ahead for your future should be a daily practice. You have to be conscious of the theory of *cause and effect.* What you cause to happen today will affect the outcome of tomorrow.

We all have planned for something at one time in our lives. It could have been a school dance or an office meeting. Planning is simply a method of doing something that is worked out in advance.

Write down your plans and the route you need to take to get to your dream. Follow through on your plans, which may mean you will need to adjust or change something in your life. Believe in yourself. Network in the right circles. Don't do drugs. Know the kinds of friends to keep and the friends to let go. Stay focused and on target with your plans.

Your potential for success is substantially increased when you plan and do your homework (prepare).

"Genius is 1% inspiration and 99% perspiration. Accordingly, a genius is often merely a talented person who has done all of his or her homework."
—Thomas Edison

Plan your next six months:

*N*o one knows what tomorrow will bring, but the practice of planning ahead is always better than the wait-and-see method.

In six months, your life will have changed for the better because of the life planning that you are now beginning. Implementing life strategies and applying future planning methods today will affect the outcome of tomorrow.

Will accomplish 1st month:

_____

_____

_____

_____

_____

Accomplished 1st month:

_____

_____

_____

_____

_____

Write down notes throughout the month to review at the end of the month when you're ready to fill in your "accomplished" lines.

Notes

_____

_____

_____

_____

_____

_____

_____

_____

_____

_____

_____

Will accomplish 2nd month:

_____

_____

_____

_____

_____

Accomplished 2nd month:

_____

_____

_____

_____

_____

*W*rite down notes throughout the month to review at the end of the month when you're ready to fill in your "accomplished" lines.

Notes

_____

_____

_____

_____

_____

_____

_____

_____

_____

_____

_____

_____

_____

Will accomplish 3rd month:

_____

_____

_____

_____

_____

Accomplished 3rd month:

_____

_____

_____

_____

Write down notes throughout the month to review at the end of the month when you're ready to fill in your "accomplished" lines.

Notes

_____

_____

_____

_____

_____

_____

_____

_____

_____

_____

_____

_____

Will accomplish 4th month:

_____

_____

_____

_____

_____

Accomplished 4th month:

_____

_____

_____

_____

_____

Write down notes throughout the month to review at the end of the month when you're ready to fill in your "accomplished" lines.

Notes

_____

_____

_____

_____

_____

_____

_____

_____

_____

_____

_____

_____

_____

_____

Will accomplish 5th month:

_____

_____

_____

_____

_____

Accomplished 5th month:

_____

_____

_____

_____

_____

Write down notes throughout the month to review at the end of the month when you're ready to fill in your "accomplished" lines.

Notes

_____

_____

_____

_____

_____

_____

_____

_____

_____

_____

_____

_____

_____

Will accomplish 6th month:

_____

_____

_____

_____

_____

Accomplished 6th month:

_____

_____

_____

_____

_____

Write down notes throughout the month to review at the end of the month when you're ready to fill in your "accomplished" lines.

Notes

_____

_____

_____

_____

_____

_____

_____

_____

_____

_____

_____

_____

Journal your thoughts:

*J*ournaling your thoughts can be effective in helping you achieve the ultimate success in life. Keeping a record of your thoughts and ideas helps you to develop a positive state of mind and provides a visual of what it is you may seek to accomplish.

While there are a variety of journaling methods available for use, we will explore the use of personal, idea, and educational journals.*

- **Personal journals** assist with personal reflection and self-clarification, in addition to allowing immaterial thoughts to take physical form. Personal journal writing can best be described as the miracle of making the invisible visible. A personal journal is a written record that documents your thoughts from the simplest to the most complex. It allows you to search deep into your heart and translate your emotions onto paper, making your thoughts a reality and more tangible.
- **Idea journals** are great resources for keeping track of ideas that come to mind while driving, having lunch, or just meditating. Journaling allows you to see your path more clearly. A business plan can be considered an idea journal because it precisely defines your business, identifies your goals, and is an organized record and visible representation of the central meaning. It is the end result of an idea that has been committed to memory and has materialized by being committed to paper and put into action.
- **Educational journals** can serve as valuable tools in the education process for both teachers and students. It allows them to keep a record of progress and achievements. Students in an experimental group who wrote on three or more occasions experienced the greatest benefits. This

---

* A sample journal is provided in the back of the book.

piece of evidence, among others, supports the fact that writing can enhance one's academic abilities and creates an environment conducive to learning. Educational journals are a vehicle to reinforce the process of learning and retaining the information.

Journal Your Thoughts

Read, Think, and Ponder

Read to open up the world of entrepreneurship to you.

Think about your achievements.

Ponder your success.

One of the richest men in the world, Bill Gates, founder of Microsoft, takes two weeks out of his busy schedule biannually to read, think, and ponder the future of Microsoft. During this time, he reads different suggestions from his employees. He knows how important it is to keep up with all the things going on around him. So Mr. Gates takes this time to read up on any and all suggestions, ideas, and thoughts his employees have on how to better the company, which, in turn, will help maintain his success in business.

If Bill Gates can take the time to do this—and we all know how successful Microsoft is—we certainly can take the time to read, think, and ponder. The more Bill Gates exercises this process, the more successful he becomes.

What Microsoft is to Bill Gates is what high school is to you. Microsoft is his job and responsibility, just as high school is your job and responsibility. The more you read, think, and ponder, the more successful you will be in all areas of your life, including your high school career. These years are the preparation time for college. Absorb and learn as much as possible. This is the time to read, think, and ponder all things. You can choose simple things to practice this technique on.

Chess is a challenging game. You must think and ponder all your moves. Life is like the game of chess. You have the best chance at being a winner if you know how to play the game. Life is not a game though; nor is it a trial run or dress rehearsal. This is the real thing. So let's live the best life we can and enjoy our journey to success.

Your journey to success is like a chess game. Playing chess is all about using your common sense and thoroughly thinking through your next move. If you make a hasty, rash move, your opponent may capture one of your pieces.

In life, if you make a hasty or rash decision, you may end up putting yourself in a bad situation. Make well-thought-out moves, and anticipate what's going to happen. Every action has a reaction. Learn to make the right moves. Learn to anticipate circumstances. Develop a sixth sense. Understand that you control the outcome of the game with the moves you make.

In chess, as in life, you have to anticipate your moves and the moves of your opponent. In life, the faster you learn to make well-thought-out moves, the faster you will get on the path to success. Take responsibility.

The chess game is set up with the king and queen in the back and all the other game pieces in front and on the sides. That setup represents life. Imagine the other pieces as different obstacles in life. Those obstacles are what's between you and your goals.

Create a list of your goals. My goals are to be happy, have great friends, have financial freedom, become a successful writer, and to reach my full potential. Write a list of your goals. Put them someplace where you can view them every day. I placed my goals on the ceiling over my bed. I look at them every morning when I wake up. You want to place your goals in a place where you can view them every day. If the ceiling is not an option for you, place your goals on the mirror in your bathroom.

Create lofty goals. Do not shortchange yourself. Play chess, not checkers. Checkers is a game of moves and reactive moves. Chess is a game of well-thought-out strategic moves. Become the leader, mover, and shaker and not the reactor to other people's moves.

Budget

Without a budget, the money goes away.

With a budget, the money stays.

Making money is easy; the challenge is keeping it. You can earn $2,500.00 a month and have money left over at the end of the month, or you can earn $2,500.00 a month and be broke at the end of the month. It all depends on your budgeting skills.

The first rule of budgeting is to create a budget every time you get money. Most people get paid weekly or every two weeks. Either way, make sure you do not pay anything until you figure out your budget. When preparing your budget, remember to include miscellaneous items, such as movies, dining out, gifts, and emergency funds (doctor bills, car repairs, etc.). You may budget all the reoccurring bills monthly and still be in the negative because of miscellaneous items—if you fail to include them.

Another important item to add to the budget is the savings column. This savings column is where you pay yourself each month. Always pay yourself in each budget. Put that money into a savings account, and watch it grow, month after month. What a great way to develop the habit of saving. If it becomes difficult to save that way, start to think of the savings account as an outstanding debt that needs to be paid monthly. Do whatever works for you, just be sure you save.

Let's get started with a sample list of things you need to pay before getting your next check.

Rent/mortgage	500.00
Utilities	75.00
Vehicle payments	200.00
Car insurance	100.00
Car maintenance (e.g. oil changes, tire rotations)	75.00
Debt (credit card payments)	100.00
Gas	65.00
Tuition, school supplies	175.00
Food/groceries	135.00
Health insurance	82.00
Total	1,512.00

No matter the state of your personal finances, whether you're wealthy or poor or somewhere in between, take time to create a budget. Set goals when you make the budget. Determine what you want to accomplish. Work a little toward your goals every day. It's much easier to achieve goals when you focus on the individual steps toward them.

This all sounds a little bit overwhelming, but your financial itinerary will be enhanced. Developing good budgeting skills early in life will help you to keep track of all your hard-earned money.

Tick Tock, Don't Stop

Time is very important, and it is not endless. There are twenty-four hours in a day and seven days in a week. You can only do so many things in that time frame. Use your time wisely, and never waste a moment.

When you own your own business, you're not restricted to a nine-to-five time frame. An entrepreneur has options regarding time; you can utilize the entire twenty-four hours in the day and the entire seven days in the week. Generally, in the beginning stages of creating your empire, you will utilize many hours of the day.

You should stop your day to enjoy ten minutes of quiet time. Having some free time to yourself will improve your effectiveness when you are working and will help you to find and unleash your creative juices.

The more quality time you put toward your business, the faster the business will progress. No time restrictions are placed on you when you're in control of the business. Of course, there will be deadlines to meet, but it's not within a nine-to-five time frame. Having free time allows you to do other things, things that you enjoy.

Building your empire as an entrepreneur is an exciting career that can provide many wonderful benefits. Independence, flexibility, and the opportunity to earn an excellent living are just a few. Many professions require degrees or advanced degrees. Becoming an entrepreneur does not require either. Although it may not require a degree to become an entrepreneur, obtaining your degree or degrees is most certainly a tremendous benefit.

As you will read later in the book, becoming educated is extremely important. Remember to stay focused and learn to balance distractions. You can spend that time on growing your company.

Stay focused. Once you have made the decision to begin to create your empire, you cannot become distracted. Anything that interferes with your concentration on your goal is a distraction, and, remember, distractions are costly.

Plan ahead. Write down five things that would be distractions for you. On one side, write the distraction, and on the other side, write your solution.

Distraction	**Solution**
_____	_____
_____	_____
_____	_____
_____	_____
_____	_____

Seize the
Opportunity

An opportunity is the chance to do something for advancement.

You never want to miss out on any good opportunities. Always be prepared, willing, and able to do something. Have any tools that you will need ready in advance. Success equals opportunity meeting preparedness.

> *"Use yesterday to build on today for the benefit of tomorrow." —Ellen Sue Burton, publisher, DUO magazine*

Your future starts *today*. The beautiful thing about a new day is the fact it's also a new beginning. It does not matter how you started the first part of your life or how you started the day, every day is a new day, which allows for a new beginning.

Start preparing by taking the necessary steps to put your ideas into action. There is a catalyst to everything. Every action has a reaction. Always remember, a thought is a catalyst for an idea, and your reaction to your idea should be positive motivation to take action.

Never procrastinate or become stagnant with your ideas. Use your ideas and thoughts; keep them in the forefront. Don't let them sit; otherwise, you will never know the opportunities that putting your thoughts into action will afford you.

We will all get opportunities in life; the key is to know which opportunities to seize. Use these steps to identify good opportunities.

- Keep an open mind. You don't have to jump at everything that is presented to you, but learn to listen to many of the ideas that are presented. Not everything will come in a conventional way. Some of your best opportunities may come from the most *unconventional* sources.
- The Internet has opened the world up to all of us. Learn how to properly utilize the World Wide Web to your advantage.

Utilize Your Talents

*T*alent is a personal gift or skill. A gift is a natural ability that you're born having. A skill is the ability to do something well; it is usually gained through training or experience. Whether you're born with it or trained for it, always utilize your talents and skills.

We all have a talent that is unique to us. The earlier we discover what our talents are, the greater the opportunity we will have to fully develop those talents. Some discover they have natural talent and others discover that their talent needs to be fine-tuned. Once your talent comes to light, remember to learn as much as possible, practice your gift continuously, and implement your skill.

There is a phrase that states "A mind is a terrible thing to waste." That phrase is apropos for this topic. As with the mind, gifts, talents, and skills are also terrible things to waste. For those of us who have discovered ours, we are fortunate. Not everyone is so lucky. So, for those of you who have not quite yet tapped into your gifts, talents, and skills, let's talk a little about how to discover them.

- Have an open mind. Do not be afraid to discover your talent.
- Take notice of what comes naturally to you, what things are effortless to you. Natural given talent is a talent that is not only beneficial to you but to other people too.
- Make a list of the things that you have mastered over the years. Use self-observation and honesty to create the list.

- Write down the things that you love to do, the things that you would do with or without pay.
- Try taking various personality tests. Check the Internet for various sites that offer personality testing.
- Keep a journal. It does not have to be anything fancy or detailed. Jot down things at different times of the day to keep track of your daily activities. If you're not much of a writer, you can do an exercise called mind mapping. Describe: regardless of the method you choose to use, make sure you capture your thoughts from time to time.

Once you have identified your talent, nurture and develop that talent. Be passionate; believe in your talent, and pursue your dream. Developing your talent will enhance your chances of creating a very successful entrepreneurial organization.

Traditional employers are now incorporating a variety of personality testing and surveys as a part of the hiring process. These tests can determine a particular gift, talent, or skill that a prospective employee may exhibit, thereby allowing for appropriate placement within their company.

A person who exhibits a high level of skill or talent in the marketing section would not serve your business well if he or she were placed in the accounting department. That person's talent would be better used in the sales or advertising department. As an entrepreneur, it is important to implement the same variety of personality testing during the interview and/or hiring process to ensure you maximize the gifts, talents, or skills of those directed to work as employees or partners within your entrepreneurial organization.

Cyber etiquette

The Internet is transportation medium over which data pockets are transmitted. In today's modern terms, it is sometimes referred to as the information highway but more commonly as just "the Internet." This medium exploded in growth in the early 1990s when Tim Berners-Lee developed the http protocol, allowing users to access and link information together; exchanges of information could then be realized.

In the beginning, universities adapted to the usage of the Internet. Before long, tech wizards with an entrepreneurial spirit realized a commercial application of this form could make millions if not *billions* of dollars.

In early 2000, almost all medium to large companies had a presence on the Web. By 2005, the cost of a PC or personal computer became so affordable to the average person that a majority of the households today now have a personal computer with access to the World Wide Web. Adults and children enjoy the usage of the Internet, but along with this privilege come rules and responsibilities. Therefore, cyber etiquette was established.

Etiquette in any shape or form is most important. We live in a world of advanced technology, in an age of instant communication where we can send a message anywhere in the world in a matter of seconds. We communicate via e-mails, text messages, and instant messaging (IM). We basically live in the world of the Internet, also known as cyberspace. Information can be obtained quite easily through the Internet. People look for friends and search for lost relatives, and employers post job positions and seek qualified applicants via e-mail applications.

Please note that just as employers post positions on the Internet, they also seek applications from the Internet. The employer will view your MySpace, Facebook, and other social-networking sites that you may be involved with. *Do not* post anything on these sites that you would not want the world to see. Your posting may hinder you from getting a job. If you have pictures of yourself with drinks in hand or appearing totally out of control, your employer may think that's the real you and not hire you. Only post pictures and messages that are appropriate and reflect positively on you.

Entrepreneurs go on to the Internet to search the World Wide Web, or as it's commonly called "the Web," for an array of opportunities. The entrepreneur will communicate with individuals from all over the world. Today, even doctors consult other doctors around the world to perform certain procedures and prescribe medications in cases of unknown diagnoses. However, all this communication must be in a manner that is professionally and ethically correct. There are different types of cyber etiquettes depending on the type of communication and, of course, the people with whom you're communicating.

E-mail is generally considered an informal way of communicating. However, when using business e-mail as a form of communication, you must establish the right tone and use the right wording. For example, write your e-mail as if you were talking face-to-face with the recipient. Imagine for a moment that you are face-to-face with a co-worker. Certainly, you would talk one way. However, if you were face-to-face with the CEO of your company, you would speak differently.

Before you begin any type of cyber communication via the Web, think about how you would interact with someone in real life. The same etiquette would apply here in cyberspace. The tone of your communication will be dictated by the manner of your interaction. Ask yourself: Who is my reader? What is my relationship to this reader? Most important, what do I wish to convey to my reader and have my reader do as a result of my e-mail?

In order to gauge the formality of your communication, you should consider the previous questions seriously.

You create different voices by changing your level of language. Your e-mail can range from formal to conversational to just plain friendly.

E-mail Etiquette—Setting a Formal Tone
- Begin with "Dear (name of person)."
- Address the reader by title (Mr., Ms., Dr.).
- Use formal, respectful language.
- Don't use contractions (e.g., use "you would," instead of "you'd").
- Use objective words and with specific terminology.
- Close with the words "Sincerely or "Yours truly," and your name and job title.

E-mail Etiquette—Setting a Conversational Tone
- Begin with an informal greeting with the reader's first name, such as "Hi" or "Hello (name)."
- Use a friendly but professional tone.
- Use some contractions ("I'm" instead of "I am").
- Keep the message light, based on a connection between you and your reader.
- Have a brief, friendly closing, using your first name only and your job title if applicable, but only if you feel it necessary to relay your title as a matter of importance.

E-mail Etiquette—Setting a Friendly Tone
- Start with a casual greeting, such as "Hi (name)."
- Use contractions ("can't" instead of "cannot").

- Use appropriate humor.
- Use jargon and slang as long as it doesn't become unprofessional.
- Use a casual closing with your first name only, no job title.

Additional Technology Etiquette Tips:

- Avoid using e-mail for personal and sensitive messages. They can easily be misinterpreted because of a lack of vocal tone and body-language cues.
- Cell phones should be turned off during business meetings, seminars, or any formal gathering where the speaker is seeking our undivided attention.

Cyber ethics has become an important topic for elementary school children, high school students, university and college students, and those in the workplace in recent years. The treatment of what is said to be cyber ethical behavior may vary from place to place.

Perhaps the most important principles created for the subject and the use of cyber ethics can be found in a list of cyber commandments available from the Computer Ethics Institute—most commonly known as the "Thou Shall Not" acts. Listed below are some of these commandments.

Thou shall not...
appropriate other people's intellectual property (IP).

Thou shall not...
ignore the social and legal consequences related to the software program one is writing or the computer system one is designing.

Thou shall not...
illegally copy or use proprietary software that has not been paid for or for which credit has not been given

Thou shall not...
interfere with others' computers or online work.

Thou shall not...
snoop into or alter others' computer files or data.

Thou shall not...
use a computer to bear false witness.

Thou shall not...
use a computer to cause harm to others.

Thou shall not...
use others' computer resources without prior authorization.

Thou shall not...
use the computer in ways that ignore the consideration of and respect for fellow human beings

by the **Computer Ethics Institute**

Journal Your Thoughts

MySpace, Facebook, Twitter, and LinkedIn

We now live in the twenty-first century, often referred to as the age of information, because that is exactly what it is. Now, more than ever, information is readily available and easily accessed. This is a fact that we have become more aware of every day in both our public and personal lives. Social networking is fueling a new trend in Internet usage.

There have been several web sites dedicated to social networking. These sites are meant to connect people using the various resources of the World Wide Web. Web sites, such as MySpace, Facebook, Twitter, and LinkedIn, among others, have made it possible for millions of people to be connected with the click of a mouse.

As with any other public forum, these networking sites have their own ups and downs. Be careful when joining any social network, particularly through the e-mail invite process. You will receive an invite from a friend in your e-mail address to join a network. This is a very easy way for fraudulent individuals to have a drastic impact on your privacy and the security of your computer.

When you decide to join one of these sites, there is certain information the site will require in order to allow membership.

Most often, these sites ask for a valid e-mail address, educational background, and sometimes political or religious preferences, all of which may be on display for the whole world to see. This is the center of controversy for many groups. Some believe that there should be a limit to what and how much information is actually available to strangers. This is a fact that users must actively be aware of because they do not know who is viewing the information that is being posted.

Profiles on these Web sites many times have valuable information about individuals. Some sites may sell your information to various companies without your knowledge. Often, prospective employers will use a person's Web page as an additional reference. So it would be in your best interest to monitor what you are uploading to these sites.

These social networks can be a lot of fun and allow you to connect with your friends and family from around the world. Sometimes it's easier to turn on your computer than pick up the phone. Enjoy the social networking sites, but also be aware of the pitfalls.

Leaving Your
Footprint

From the time you were born, you began to have experiences that enabled you to grow in life. Almost every experience you have can provide life lessons. Some are small, and some are large; nevertheless, they are lessons. You must keep an open mind and a willingness to learn from your experiences. You can learn and grow, or you can resist learning and struggle throughout life. Embracing the situation and learning from it is always the best way to go. As you conquer your experiences and move on to the next life lesson, you will leave a footprint.

As we go through life, we all leave footprints. Good or bad, we leave them. These footprints are life lessons; they include your experiences, your struggles, and your accomplishments. Your goal is to leave good footprints. There is always someone who is coming behind you. It could be a sibling, cousin, classmate, or friend. You want to create a good path for the next person. In order to do this, you must live your life to the best of your ability. Finding your own lessons from the events in your life is a skill that improves with practice. Learn to take a minute to stop and reflect on different situations in your life and meditate on the course of action to take.

As they say, if life gives you lemons, make lemonade. Take what you have, work with it, and make the best of it. The more lemons you get, the more lemonade you will make and the better you will get at making lemonade. The better you get, the more you can share with friends and classmates.

The ability to take the bad and turn it into good is a quality that you will need to acquire early, if you want to be successful at life. Never wallow in self-pity or give up. If you fail at something, get up and try again and again until you get it right. That is the trait of a winner.

Some shoes are a little big to fill, and the idea of leaving such a footprint may be a little overwhelming. Some think it would be hard to follow the footprints of a Tiger Woods or a Michael Phelps. That's not true; you can follow their dedication, sacrifice, motivation, and winning spirit. You can apply these traits to your personal journey to success and leave your footprints for the next person to follow.

- Never give up on anything.
- Life is what you make it.
- Get lemons, make lemonade.
- Choose to be happy.
- It's never too late to be who you could have been.
- Never lose yourself in someone else's shadow.
- If you have a sibling who seems to be a hard act to follow, make your own act.

"Some people come into our lives and quickly go. Some stay for awhile and leave footprints on our hearts. And we are never, ever the same." —*Anonymous*

Profile of Dwyane Wade Sr.

A *native of Chicago, Dwyane Wade Sr.* enjoyed working with youth in the sports, academic, and mentoring fields, which led to him becoming the CEO and founder of the Pro Pops Foundation.

His life is dedicated to assisting youth, from adolescence to adulthood, in obtaining and maintaining adequate knowledge in education and athletics, so they will be able to become self-sufficient and productive members of society.

Mr. Wade began his early education at Ryder Elementary School on the south side of Chicago. He went on to graduate from Sieom High School, where his love of sports was developed and nurtured. He was an all-around athlete and played on the football, baseball, wrestling, and volleyball teams. Even though the volleyball team was traditionally an all-girls team, that did not hinder his desire to play the game. He was not able to convince any of the other boys to play on the all-girls team with him, but his passion for sport far outweighed his reservation about being the only boy on the team. He would play any sport that was available at the high school. He has always had and continues to have a competitive spirit. He trains his mind as well as his body to perform at its highest ability.

Mr. Wade joined the military as a teenager and took on the sport of boxing, at which he excelled. He was featured on the *Wide*

World of Sports in 1977. He went on to complete his education at Florida State University in Tallahassee, Florida. Upon graduation, he became a dedicated and established teacher of athletics via academics. He is known in the community for always going above and beyond to help others achieve their goals, from enhancing their athletic skills to developing their minds, and to know their worth as human beings.

As founder and CEO of the Pro Pops Foundation, Mr. Wade wants to leave his footprint for those to come. The foundation coordinates functions and fundraisers to assist in creating youth athletic, academic, and mentoring programs. His tireless efforts are all directed toward enhancing the lives of all youth.

Dwyane Sr. utilizes all avenues available to him as a way of giving back to society and as a vehicle to provide youth with a positive medium to becoming productive members of society, along with the fulfillment that can be achieved from being secure and self-assured individuals.

Mr. Wade has mentored many and hopes that he has given as much to those that he has had the pleasure of coming in contact with as he has received in fulfillment.

Through Mr. Wade's teaching in his Pro Pops camp, he focuses on helping the kids to understand the impact of intelligence on an individual's ability to succeed in society. The early foundation of learning allows the youth to understand the correlations between acquiring, retaining, and applying this knowledge toward success. It's like a mathematical equation: learning + applying = success.

Dwyane Sr. now lives in South Florida, but he continues to travel the country making an impact on kids and leaving a footprint for others to follow.

Your turn

Profile

Create your profile:

I was born _____

_____

I dedicate my life to _____

_____

_____

My educational background _____

_____

_____

Joining the following organizations has _____

_____

_____

List organizations

1. _____

2. _____

3. _____

Work history _____

_____

_____

Mentoring is something that I _____

_____

_____

Write your profile as it would be five years from now:

I was born _____

_____

I dedicate my life to _____

_____

_____

My educational background _____

_____

_____

Joining the following organizations has _____

_____

_____

List organizations

1._____

2._____

3._____

Work history _____

_____

_____

Mentoring is something that I _____

_____

_____

Entrepreneur tip:

Always live by the rules

Bill Gates' Ten Rules of Life

Rule 1: Life is not fair…get used to it.

Rule 2: The world won't care about your self-esteem. The world will expect you to accomplish something before you feel good about yourself.

Rule 3: You will *not* make $40,000 a year right out of high school. You won't be a vice president with a car phone, until you earn both.

Rule 4: .If you think your teacher is tough, wait till you get a boss. He doesn't have tenure.

Rule 5: Flipping burgers is not beneath your dignity. Your grandparents had a different word for burger flipping; they called it opportunity.

Rule 6: If you mess up, it's not your parents' fault, so don't whine about our mistakes, learn from them.

Rule 7: Before you were born, your parents weren't as boring as they are now. They got that way from paying your bills, cleaning your clothes, and listening to you talk about how cool you are. So before you save the rain forest from the parasites of your parents' generation, try "delousing" the closet in your own room.

Rule 8: Your school may have semesters and summer break. In real life, you will not have a semester and summer break. You will have to work all year long.

Rule 9: Your school may have done away with winners and losers, but life has not. In some schools, they have abolished failing grades; they'll give you as many times as you want to get the right answer. This doesn't bear the slightest resemblance to anything in real life.

Rule 10: Television is *not* real life. In real life, people actually have to leave the coffee shop and go to jobs.

Find Your Niche

Find your niche and follow it. With the advent of the Internet, you can find out what the public wants. It's not always necessary to be the first to fulfill a need for the public, but it is essential to be the person who can best fulfill that need. You don't have to reinvent the wheel, just make the wheel better. Find a business you can pour your heart and soul into and research it to become more knowledgeable on the subject. Ask yourself these questions:

- Is there a need for the product?
- How many people are searching the Web each month for the product? Do this by using Word tracker.

Develop the product, and soar in your business.

You cannot be an expert at everything, so become an expert at some things. Some of the things that will help you find your niche are things that you can learn yourself. Focus on what your skills are; know what you are passionate about. This will greatly improve your chances of becoming successful. Getting involved with something that does not hold your interest is not good. You are setting yourself up for a lifetime of boredom. You may make a lot of money, but you won't be completely fulfilled. Wouldn't it be better to know your product and believe in it, make money, and be fulfilled at the same time?

Create your niche in a strong market if possible. Be unique. That gives you some leverage. Don't go out and start a sunglasses business for parrots. Don't be that unique, but do find something that every person, household, and business will need or want to use.

- Make a list of five of your interests.
- Check the Internet for the latest Web searches and hot topics.
- Pay attention to conversations with folks you meet or already know.
- Scan your bookshelves and make a note of which reference books you have purchased or read over the years, and determine which subjects interest you.

My Interests

1. _____

2. _____

3. _____

4. _____

5. _____

"It is better to do 4 things 400 times, and master those 4 things, than to do 400 things 4 times and master none." —

Build Your Strengths

Your strength is an ability that allows you to progress toward achieving a goal or reaching a higher standard. Develop your strengths by improving on the following:

Intelligence—Read, learn, study, and seek knowledge.

Courage—Display perseverance and the ability to overcome all obstacles.

Imagination—Be innovative. Create goals, and make plans. Have vision.

Honesty—Display integrity, morals, and truthfulness.

Broad-mindedness—Think outside the box; be diverse.

Competency—Base your decisions on reason and moral principles.

Humility—Be modest and respectful.

Listening skills—Learn to concentrate on what's being said, in order to better process the information in your brain.

2 Ears 1 Mouth

We were created with two ears and one mouth for a reason. We should listen twice as much as we talk. Being a good listener not only helps you solve many problems at work or home but allows you to see the world through the eyes of others. Have you ever missed out on the details of a conversation or been told that you are not a good listener? Becoming a good listener is not difficult. Here are a few tips:

- Look at the person who is speaking to you.
- Do not interrupt.
- Give your full attention.
- Respond verbally and nonverbally (body language).
- Don't change the subject.
- Be patient and respect pauses.

A big part of being an effective businessperson is being a good listener. Keep an open mind in order to absorb knowledge. Become a broad-minded or open-minded individual. Remember this: a mind is like a parachute; if it's not open, it's not going to work. How much simpler can that be?

A good communicator is often a good listener. Once you have listened intently, respond effectively. Ask empowering questions. Don't be afraid to ask appropriate questions. By appropriate, I mean questions that pertain directly to your conversation or subject matter.

A person is not going to reveal to you personal or successful ideas until he or she gets to know you a little better. This is where building that relationship is so important. Above all, remember we have two ears and one mouth. Listen to what the other person has to say before you speak.

Jump In and Get Your Feet Wet

In order to become an entrepreneur, you just need to do it. Jump in and get your feet wet. Be willing to take on a challenge. Don't let fear paralyze your ability to become a successful entrepreneur. Feel secure and confident in yourself. Have a strong vision of the future. Know your goals, and believe vigorously in them.

> *"The way to get started is to quit talking and begin doing."*
> —*Walt Disney*

We learn from trial and error, and that includes you—you've got to live life, step into the midst of things, and try. If you fail, learn from your mistakes and stand up again. The question is not whether you will or will not make mistakes—you will—the question is whether you want to learn and grow or shrink back and be stuck. Take that step you have been avoiding. You can succeed, or you can get feedback that it did not work, but in either case, you are sure to feel alive. You may have some trials and tribulations as you start your business, but remember, struggle builds character. Be of good character, and be proud of yourself.

Learn to trust your instincts. We all have the ability to discern good from bad and right from wrong. Some tap into this instinct early; some tap into this instinct late;

> *"Things may come to those who wait, but only the things left by those who hustle."*
> *—Abraham Lincoln*

and some never tap into this trait. Develop good characteristics. A person's observable behavior is an indication of his/her character.

Find something you love to do; research it, develop it, and the money will follow.

Entrepreneur tip:

Debt is not your friend avoid excessively using credit cards.

Journal Your Thoughts

Get Your Swagger On

*A*long *with excellent credit, business savvy and wisdom are essential in becoming an entrepreneur. In other words, get your business swagger on.*

Business savvy is vital in creating and maintaining a successful business empire. A savvy businessman or businesswoman is concerned with the facts of the situation. He or she must be good at solving problems and managing matters and at dealing with difficulties.

Business savvy is having hunger and aggressiveness in business, never taking no for an answer. If a door opens, avail yourself of the opportunity with business know-how. Become shrewd, practical, well informed, and clever or sharp in practical affairs. Become a *savant,* and you will excel in business.

Business wisdom is the ability to make sensible decisions and judgments based on personal knowledge and personal experience. Your personal knowledge consists of things that you have learned throughout your life, things that you may have picked up during your daily activities. Your personal experience consists of the different things that may have happened to you or to others around you during your daily walk through your life. We are constantly learning. As we continue to live life, we also continue to learn from our experiences. From our experiences, we gain wisdom. Business wisdom is creating your own unique style. You can emulate others, but it is always better to have your own style and savvy.

Strive to become a Renaissance man or woman. Ignite your inner skills and the growing knowledge inside of you.

Light the eternal flame of knowledge inside you; it cannot be extinguished, only admired.

Part Two

Rich in Business

*T*ake the following quick test to see if you have the innate ability to become an entrepreneur.

Entrepreneur Test

1. I like to do impulsive things.   T or F

2. It is important that I receive lots of rest.   T or F

3. I like to know the outcome of a situation
   before I begin to do it.   T or F

4. I like to follow the traditional way of
   doing things.   T or F

5. I enjoy doing the same thing over and over.   T or F

6. I am a creative problem solver.   T or F

7. I like to be wild, free, and uninhibited.   T or F

8. I invest in books that help to improve my life.   T or F

9. When it's time to begin a task, I procrastinate.   T or F

10. I can identify a good business opportunity.   T or F

This is not a scientific test. If more than half of your answers were true, you have the skills to be an entrepreneur.

Entrepreneurs

*A*nyone *can become an entrepreneur.* Becoming a successful entrepreneur requires certain attributes. Most successful entrepreneurs have a few things in common. Here are some of the traits you must have or attain through repetition. You should have:

1. A creative mind
2. Resourcefulness
3. Accountability
4. The ability to take risks
5. Initiative
6. Industriousness
7. Open-mindedness
8. Drive
9. Perseverance
10. Dedication

You need to have a strong, *relentless* desire to succeed. The ability to *self-sacrifice* is required. Here's an example. You have a project you're working on, and a friend requests your presence at his birthday party. You're on a deadline for this project, and you have committed yourself. You need to be able to use one of your personality traits and make a wise decision. This trait happens to be common sense—the ability to reason through a problem and come up with the best and most appropriate answer for your friend and for the project.

Some of the other traits *required* are the willingness to deviate from traditional ways of doing things. For example, if Joe and Trevor always travel the same scenic route home day after day, they should be willing to take a highway route some days. They're arriving at the same place; they're just getting there a different way and, we hope, more efficiently.

The difference between the average person and a successful entrepreneur in the above example is the average person just continues to do things in the same manner day after day after day. A successful entrepreneur, however, will search for a better and more efficient way to do the same task with a better outcome.

Write down five different ideas that you have for a business. Remember, most successful businesses start with a need for the product or service.

1. _____

_____

_____

_____

_____

2. _____

_____

_____

_____

_____

3. _____

_____

_____

_____

_____

4._____

_____

_____

_____

_____

5._____

_____

_____

_____

_____

Entrepreneurs...

Effective—produce results

No fear—have the tenacity to do the job

Talented—have an exceptional, natural ability to do something

Relentless—never stop

Exceptional—show ability well above average

Persistent—continue despite problems

Resourceful—are full of initiative and good at problem solving

Eager—are enthusiastic and excited about doing something

Noble—have excellent moral principles and character

Educated—gather as much information as possible

Uninhibited—do not succumb to constraints

Refined—possess a high degree of precision and effectiveness

The following is a small list of entrepreneurial jobs available to you. Each person on this list has the same entrepreneurial traits.

1. Mortgage broker

2. Real estate sales associate

3. Registered appraiser

4. Radio host

5. Car detailer

6. Actor/actress

7. Singer

8. Beautician

9. Restaurant owner

10. Magazine owner

11. Barber

12. Masseuse

13. Personal trainer

14. _____

15. _____

16. _____

17. _____

18. _____

19. _____

20. _____

The Five W's

What

What is your entrepreneurial quest? Write a business plan or just jot down your goals. Develop your strategy.

When

The time is now. Don't waste any time on what-ifs and if-onlys. Why put off what you want to do today for tomorrow? Tomorrow is not guaranteed.

Where

Anywhere and everywhere in the country and all over the globe.

Why

You must consider the future in all things that you do. All your actions create reactions. No action produces no results. Begin to establish your foundation toward creating a successful empire.

How

You begin with thinking about your future. Set goals. Establish good credit. You will be ready to create your empire.

Journal Your Thoughts

Bankable Facts

*H*ere are some facts you need to know. If you don't have a bank account, open a checking and savings account. Most banks or savings and loans will have accounts that will suit your needs. If you are under eighteen years of age, Bank of America has "Student Banking 101," which is a student account that is free for five years.

After opening your bank account, turn your attention to your credit. Get on the Internet and retrieve a copy of your credit report. If your credit is brand new, you will need to follow the instructions in the credit section of this book. If your credit has a negative credit rating, you will need to contact your creditors and attempt to negotiate a payment plan or payoff settlement. As your credit issues are being worked through, turn your attention to saving money.

Take a percentage of your salary and pay yourself every pay period. Your savings account will begin to increase. Set a goal of an amount of money to save for your first venture. When your goal is reached and your credit is good, you're ready to begin the process of creating your empire.

Credit, Credit, Credit

Good credit is essential when creating a new business and starting your adult life. Credit is the pay-later system, which is an arrangement by which a buyer can take possession of something now and pay for it later or over a period of time.

Your credit determines your financial status and/or your financial reputation. A financial institution will lend you money based on your credit reputation.

When you are shopping at the mall and are a little short on cash, your credit will determine your spending entitlement at that store. You may have been with your parents and overheard the cashier ask if they wanted to apply for instant credit. That's when your credit reputation really counts.

If your credit is evaluated and determined to be acceptable, the instant credit will be granted. Once granted an amount of credit, you must follow the repayment conditions. The payment record will be recorded. If you pay your credit account thirty days late, a thirty-day late report will be recorded on your credit report. If you pay your credit account sixty days late, a sixty-day late report will be recorded; and if you pay your account ninety days late, you will have a very detrimental mark on your credit. A thirty-day late report is bad; a sixty-day late report is worse; a ninety-day late report is the kiss of death to your credit!

My Entrepreneurial Dream

Walking with my head held high past the clouds
Having limits within these skies is simply not allowed
When a man walked on the moon I refuse to settle downward
Reaching past these stars into galaxies that haven't even been found yet

Taking authority over my life to make sure my future reproduces
The tons of dreams and aspirations that drive me to push through it
I don't want to hide the shine in my light by being told I can't do this
Breaking through the chains of doubts that as a leader I won't prove to be fit

Chartering my imagination to fly where only eagles soar
Depositing my heart and soul into what I most respectfully adore
I am going to be somebody important one day walking through big double doors
Surrounded by other imperative people greeting me and welcoming many new ideas to explore

There will be no little U's and big I's on my dream team
Nor will I make them feel like little Indians because I am the Chief
I promise to encourage them because without them my visions are incomplete
With a humble spirit and a kind heart I will value them and hope the same would be returned to me
Never forgetting who helped me climb the mountains when they were low and then became too steep

In my mind I can see my dreams stretched out like the water in the sea

Feeling a gentle tug at my heart that there is something out there better for me

One day soon I am going to look back with a proud smile and say to my team, "My destiny came and found me."

And this will all because while in school I decided that an entrepreneur was more than just a big dream!

Written: July 27, 2011
2011©Monique Favors

The Entrepreneur
within Us

I had the great pleasure of having a conversation with retired veteran, Mr. Roy Morgan, from Hinesville, Georgia. We were having a friendly conversation, and he began to tell me about his childhood. He had been abandoned at three months old by a mother with some unspeakable problems. He was adopted into a loving family with a mother and father who loved and supported him emotionally and financially.

Tragedy struck the family when Roy was eight years old. His adoptive father was placed in an insane asylum. His father actually had Alzheimer's, but in the 1950s, that diagnosis was not available. Anyone with those symptoms was assumed to be insane. Roy had to take over and become the head of the household at such a young age. He did not know how to sit back and say, "Why me?" and feel pity for himself. He adapted to the circumstances and went into survival mode.

In the 1950s, you sank or you swam. If you wanted to eat, you had to work. He did not know it then, but his entrepreneurial skills were about to kick in at the tender age of eight years old. This indicates that people have innate entrepreneurial skills, and you never know which element will ignite them. In the case of Roy Morgan, the need for survival ignited his entrepreneurial traits.

He was short for an eight-year-old and had a small frame. So this young boy decided to go to the local barbershop and ask to rent a chair for a shoe-shine business. The barbershop owner was so impressed by this kid's tenacity that he rented him the chair. Thus, a business was born, and this little eight-year-old became an entrepreneur.

He charged two dimes per shine. Roy went on to expand his business. He hired three additional kids with their own shoe-shine boxes to work for him. Each of the three boys shined the shoes for their clients and gave one dime to Roy and kept one dime for themselves.

Roy had created his own empire and now had free time to do the things he wanted to do. He ended the story by telling me that after he established the work ethic of his hired help and made sure all the clients were happy with their service, he would leave the barbershop and go down to the local food stand and enjoy a long dog, coleslaw, and tall lemonade for two dimes. Roy was able to pay for his luxuries and help his mom with the bills with the money he was making from his shoe-shine employees at the local barbershop. He did all of this at eight years old.

This is not a fictitious story. I am proud to say that Mr. Roy Morgan is my uncle. Uncle Roy went on to join the military and served for forty years and in many wars. He still resides in Hinesville, Georgia. The purpose of this story is to show that you are never too young to create your own empire. You are never too young to learn how to become an entrepreneur. It does not take a rocket scientist to become a successful entrepreneur. In the above case, survival was the catalyst for Roy's entrepreneurship. You don't have to wait for your survival instinct to kick in to create your own empire.

Entrepreneurship is not just an individual thing; it can be generational. What you do today will affect you tomorrow. If you ignite the entrepreneurial spirit within you, you could influence your family for generations into becoming successful entrepreneurs. The question for you to answer is: what will it take to ignite your entrepreneurial spirit?

Warren Buffet: Ten Ways to Be Rich Theory

Number 1: Reinvest Your Profits

When you first make money, you may be tempted to spend it. Don't. Instead, reinvest the profits. Buffett learned this early on. In high school, he and a pal bought a pinball machine to put in a barbershop. With the money they earned, they bought more machines until they had eight in different shops. When the friends sold the venture, Buffett used the proceeds to buy stocks and to start another small business.

Number 2: Be Willing to Be Different

Don't base your decisions upon what everyone is saying or doing. When Buffett began managing money in 1956 with $100,000 cobbled together from a handful of investors, he was dubbed an oddball. He worked in Omaha, not on Wall Street, and he refused to tell his partners where he was putting their money. People predicted that he'd fail, but when he closed his partnership fourteen years later, it was worth more than $100 million.

Number 3: Never Suck Your Thumb

Gather in advance any information you need to make a decision, and ask a friend or relative to make sure that you stick to a deadline. Buffett prides himself on swiftly making up his mind and acting on it. He calls any unnecessary sitting and thinking "thumb-sucking."

Number 4: Spell Out the Deal before You Start

Your bargaining leverage is always greatest before you begin a job. That's when you have something to offer that the other party wants. Buffett learned this lesson the hard way as a kid, when his grandfather Ernest hired him and a friend to dig out the family grocery store after a blizzard. The boys spent five hours shoveling. They shoveled until they could barely straighten their frozen hands. Afterward, his grandfather gave the pair less than ninety cents to split.

Number 5: Watch Small Expenses

Buffett invests in businesses run by managers who obsess over the tiniest costs. He once acquired a company whose owner counted the sheets in rolls of five-hundred-sheet toilet paper to see if he was being cheated (he was). He also admired a friend who painted only the side of his office building that faced the road.

Number 6: Limit What You Borrow

Buffett has never borrowed a significant amount—not to invest, not for a mortgage. He has gotten many heart-wrenching letters from people who thought their borrowing was manageable but became overwhelmed by debt. His advice: negotiate with creditors to pay what you can. Then, when you're debt-free, work on saving some money that you can use to invest.

Number 7: Be Persistent

With tenacity and ingenuity, you can win against a more established competitor. Buffett acquired the Nebraska Furniture Mart in 1983 because he liked the way its founder, Rose Blumkin, did business. A Russian immigrant, she built the mart from a pawnshop into the largest furniture store in North America. Her strategy was to undersell the big shots, and she was a merciless negotiator.

Number 8: Know When to Quit

Once, when Buffett was a teen, he went to the racetrack. He bet on a race and lost. To recoup his funds, he bet on another race. He lost again, leaving him with close to nothing. He felt sick; he had squandered nearly a week's earnings. Buffett never repeated that mistake.

Number 9: Assess the Risks

In 1995, the employer of Buffett's son, Howie, was accused by the FBI of price-fixing. Buffett advised Howie to imagine the worst- and best-case scenarios if he stayed with the company. His son quickly realized that the risks of staying far outweighed any potential gains, and he quit the next day.

Number 10: Know What Success Really Means

Despite his wealth, Buffett does not measure success by dollars. In 2006, he pledged to give away almost his entire fortune to charities, primarily the Bill and Melinda Gates Foundation. He's adamant about not funding monuments to himself—no Warren Buffett buildings or halls. "When you get to my age, you'll measure your success in life by how many of the people you want to have love you actually do love you. That's the ultimate test of how you've lived your life."

Sweat Equity

Sweat equity is the human contribution to a business, the time and knowledge that an individual puts into the business to make a result. It's all the hard work to start up a business. It's also all the hard work that is put into developing the business to another level.

Sweat equity can best be explained in real estate. When people make repairs on their homes, upgrade the windows, or add a patio, those are all improving the value of their home. They increased their home's value by their own efforts. Their home was appraised at one value, and once the upgrades were completed, the home appraised at a higher value. The difference between these two values is the sweat equity.

When starting up a business, sweat equity will become a large part of the business. You may not have much capital, but you do have your time and knowledge, which is priceless. Put as much of yourself into your business as possible to enhance your chance of success.

When determining the value of the sweat equity that would be provided to your business from employees or potential investors, you should consider the following characteristics.

- *Commitment* to the success of the business.
- What *unique contributions* will that person bring to the business?
- Are the *hopes, dreams, and aspirations* of the person similar to yours.

The sweat equity that is created in your company as a direct result of hard work, training, and learning is the sweat equity. The more training and knowledge that you receive in your profession, the better the chances are that you will succeed tremendously. You will always succeed; the height of success is determinate upon the training, knowledge, and hard work you put in to your company. Paying your dues is another type of sweat equity. The earlier you pay your dues, the quicker you can move on to building your empire.

Sweat equity is also a factor in education. Just showing up daily for class and expecting to develop yourself into a good student and have great success in that class is not realistic. True success is showing up for class and being an active participant in class. If you want to get a great return on all your efforts, you must work hard, develop great study habits, participate, and pay attention in class. The return that you will receive is an A in the class. The sweat equity was all the hard work that you did to achieve the greatest results.

Entrepreneur Tip:

Do not get a mortgage on a home.

Go to <u>www.browardrealforeclose.com</u> and bid for your home.

Journal Your Thoughts

The State of the Economy

We are now experiencing an economic slowdown, with our job and housing markets being greatly affected. Your parents are the affected majority. The responsibilities of your parents are to clothe, feed, and shelter you. That's becoming increasingly difficult as the economy continues to slow down.

Unfortunately, these circumstances are not invisible to those in the adolescent stage in life. Young adults are now finding themselves having to take on a part-time job in order to have extra money for their wants.

For example, your parents will provide your school necessities, but you will provide the funds for the iPod to listen to on the bus. Parents may have to supplement their income with part-time jobs on top of the full-time jobs they already have, just to maintain the status quo. Your responsibility is to learn from your parents' influence, work diligently in school, and not allow the circumstances of the economy to affect your aspirations of success in your adulthood.

Whether the economy is booming or in a slowdown, stay focused and do not be discouraged by the economic situation. *Be aware but not fearful.* You can be in control of the outcome of your success in any type of economy.

Find the positive in all situations and take advantage of the slowdown. In the words of the rapper Jay-Z, "Brush your shoulders off" and keep it moving. Do not let anything deter you from your goal of success. If you're faced with a challenge, think on it, learn about it, and conquer it. Remember that having to struggle a little is common on the road to success. *Struggle builds character.*

Typically in an economic slowdown, real estate is a great investment. The price of homes has been reduced tremendously in this slowdown, which allows for much profit once the market turns around. Foreclosed homes are priced at an all-time low. A foreclosure is a legal proceeding by which the bank seeks through the courts to regain all rights to a property, due to nonpayment by the homeowner. When the bank legally regains possession of the property, it will entertain offers from individuals seeking to purchase the property for what was owed.

The appraised value is what the property is worth in comparison to other properties in the immediately surrounding areas. If the appraised value is $100,000 and the loan amount was $40,000, the bank may sell to an individual for the $40,000 owed to the bank, which would leave $60,000 in equity for the new homeowner. If the homeowner decided to sell for the appraised value, the homeowner would walk away with $60,000. Not bad for a few months of work!

Acquiring real property is always a good way to build upon your success. There are many other entrepreneurial ventures you can go into based on what the economy is doing. This was just one example.

In my opinion, land is one of the most profitable investments you can make. Your profit margin with land has the potential to be enormous. As an example, you can purchase land at a county auction for pennies on the dollar. Hold on to the land until the equity builds up and then sell.

If you purchase for $5,000.00 for a quarter acre and sell for $20,000.00 a quarter acre, you have made a substantial profit. Remember when you're selling, as an investor, always leave some room in the sale for the buyer to make a profit when the buyer chooses to sell. As an investor, you want to have repeat and referred customers. To make this happen, your buyers must trust you to sell to them at the wholesale price. The wholesale price means a price for the purpose of resale with a profit.

> *"He who is not courageous enough to take risks will accomplish nothing in life."*— Maya Angelou

Buy land with no credit requirements and low down payments. Land is one of the best types of investment to make. Land is controlled, immovable. Man cannot produce more land. It is what it is. The world is constantly growing in population. As a result of this growth, more and more housing is required; therefore, land has become a precious commodity. As land becomes less and less and the demand becomes more and more, the value greatly increases. The land in South Florida is far more expensive than the land in Central Florida. That is due to the demand for land in South Florida, because land cannot be reproduced. Land is just one of many opportunities available to you as an entrepreneur.

There are many different ways to invest your money and get a return on it. You can invest in land, foreclosures, tax certificates, tax deed sales, real property, and even yourself. Investing in land has advantages over investing in real property. When you own a home, you have the worry of repairs on the property and the continuous upkeep. If the property is an investment property, you have the issue of renting the property.

If you live in a state that has hurricanes, as an example, you would have to make sure the house is properly secured against the storms and hurricanes. Land, on the other hand, is very low maintenance. Most of the work in the purchase of land is done on the front end. Some of the things you would want to do is have a soil treatment test done. Also survey the land to learn where the boundaries of your property are.

These are just a few examples of what you would need to do to become a successful landowner. Remember, do not allow the state of the economy to affect your success. Choose a business that will serve the majority of the public and success will follow. The key is to find the business that fits the time we are living in or that will be required in the near future.

Entrepreneur tip:

Create your personal success recipe.

Journal Your Thoughts

Recipe for Business Success

1 large cup of enthusiasm

A double helping of knowledge

A pint of motivation

A gallon of wisdom

A quart of savvy

Stir it all together, and let simmer. Garnish with common sense. Season to taste.

(The ingredients may be different; however, the final dish will be the same: *Success!*)

Part Three

Rich in
Friendship

Entrepreneur tip:

In order to have a good friend, You must be a good friend

Value Your Friends

*H*aving a great support system is definitely an asset
to you as you create your empire. Having good friends
and wise mentors will help you to excel in all your goals. You
attract what you are. That means if you want a good friend, you
have to be a good friend. A friend is someone who is well known
to you, someone you like and respect. You regard this person
with trust and affection; he or she is a confidant and ally. You will
have similar likes and dislikes.

Here are a few pointers on how to be a good friend.

1. We must be *considerate*, which means be kind to one
   another. We must have patience for the next person and
   have genuine feelings of concern for our friends. Be
   respectful and loyal.

2. We must be *committed*, be devoted to the friendship. We
   must remain friends in good times and in bad times. We
   must be loyal and selfless, not selfish.

3. We must be *candid*, open, and sincere. We must refrain
   from disguise and subterfuge and speak with honesty and
   frankness.

4. We must be *constructive*, say and do things that are helpful
   to our friends, and promote further advancement. We
   should be uplifting.

5. We must be *confidential.* This means no gossiping and sharing of information told to us in secret. We must be able to hold another's trust or confidence.

6. We must be *consistent,* never wavering in the friendship, congruent, harmonious, reliable, and steady. We should be uniform in our feelings of friendship.

If you want a good friend with all the above qualities, you must be a friend who possesses all these qualities. Studies show that having a well-balanced social life helps promote a healthy outlook on life. A healthy outlook on life greatly increases your ability to become successful in life.

We do not have a choice with the family we have, but we do have control of who we choose as friends. Having a few good friends is better than having many friends you cannot rely on. The good friendships that you develop in high school and college will be with you throughout your entire life, so choose them wisely. Finding a good friend is like finding a treasure. It can make your life richer in so many ways.

- The characteristic that I embody the most:

  _____

- The characteristic that I need to work on:

  _____

Who's on Your Team

Your team is the people you have around you—those you associate with, the people you work with. Have a personal team and a professional team. A strong supportive team will help you succeed in all your endeavors. While a strong team is not mandatory to be successful, it sure makes getting there a little easier.

Personal Team
- Associate—someone who joins with you in some type of activity or endeavor.
- Acquaintance—someone who is known slightly rather than intimately.
- Confidant—someone you trust to share personal and intimate matters.
- Short-term individual—someone who is in your life for a brief moment. After they have whatever it was that they needed from you, they leave.
- Fair-weather individual—someone who is there when things are going great but steps away when things get a little difficult. They come back once the problem or situation gets resolved.
- True friend—someone who is a loyal, loving, genuine, and faithful. A committed and trusting individual who is with you through thick and thin.

"He who finds a faithful friend, finds a treasure."
—Anonymous

Haters

I wanted to share some thoughts with you about haters, and then I read this phenomenal poem. What you need to know about haters has already been established in great literary form by renowned author and poet Maya Angelou in a poem that says it all.

"A Hater" by Maya Angelou

A hater is someone who is jealous and envious and spends all their time trying to make you look small so they can look tall. They are very negative people to say the least. Nothing is ever good enough! When you make your mark, you will always attract some haters...That's why you have to be careful with whom you share your blessings and your dreams, because some folk can't handle seeing you blessed...

It's dangerous to be like somebody else...

If God wanted you to be like somebody else, He would have given you what He gave them! Right? You never know what people have gone through to get what they have.

The problem I have with haters is that they see my glory, but they don't know my story...If the grass looks greener on the other side of the fence, you can rest assured that the water bill is higher there too!

We've all got some haters among us! People envy you because you can:

Have a relationship with God

Light up a room when you walk in

Start your own business

Tell a man / woman to hit the curb (if he / she isn't about the right thing)

Raise your children without both parents being in the home Haters can't stand to see you happy, Haters will never want to see you succeed, Haters never want you to get the victory, most of our haters are people who are supposed to be on our side. How do you handle your undercover haters?

You can handle these haters by:

1. Knowing who you are & who your true friends are

2. Having a purpose to your life? Purpose does not mean having a job.

You can have a job and still be unfulfilled. A purpose is having a clear sense of what God has called you to be. Your purpose is not defined by what others think about you.

3. By remembering what you have is by divine prerogative and not human manipulation. Fulfill your dreams!

You only have one life to live...when it's your time to leave this earth, you "want" to be able to say, "I've lived my life and fulfilled 'my' dreams,... Now I'm ready to go HOME!" When God gives you favor, you can tell your haters, "Don't look at me...Look at Who is in charge of me..."

—Maya Angelou

*H*aters are people who pretend to be happy about any success you may have, but they are really jealous. They always have more negative than positive things to say about anything or anyone.

Haters will turn your good qualities around and make them look like bad qualities, just because they cannot come close to achieving the type of success you can. Haters have nothing going for them and become extremely jealous, negative, and vindictive toward others who are moving forward in life.

There are various forms of haters. They can range from those who completely dismiss any positive traits in someone to those who just have a few unkind words to say. There is no need to ever become a hater.

The world is large enough for everyone to have a completely successful life and not impede another person's success. Be supportive and encouraging of another person's success. Remember the Golden Rule: "Do unto others as you would have them do unto you." Don't hate. Learn to appreciate.

Journal Your Thoughts

Know Your Worth

*A*s *you begin to discover your gifts, talents, and skills,* *you will begin to change for the better.* An important part of change is understanding who you are and what you value. Everyone possesses the power to know his or her worth. Some individuals may not have unlocked this power. If you haven't, look deep and find the key to unlock this power.

You are somebody with gifts and talents. Know your worth. You are valuable to the world. There is only one you. *You are unique.* We all have different DNA. No two of us have the same fingerprint or the same DNA. That makes us special.

You don't need to be in a gang or have a posse, an audience, or an entourage; you just need you. Know your worth. As you walk through life, you will experience different things. Some will be valuable lessons, and others will be experiences you would rather forget.

Through these lessons, you will begin to learn where you will draw the line in certain situations. You will learn not to be influenced in a negative way. Peer pressure has negatively altered if not destroyed many young people who did not know their worth.

When you are riding in the car with your peers and someone offers you a joint or some other type of drug, you will have the courage to say no. You will say no because you know your worth and you understand that putting an illegal drug in your body could damage your health and cause you many different types of legal issues. You value your health and your freedom; you know your worth. As you continue to learn how unique you are and that you are irreplaceable, you will start to accrue successful accomplishments.

Knowing your worth is understanding your importance. You are an unlimited being. There is nothing that you cannot achieve. The only limits you have are the limits that you impose on yourself. The gift of birth is a miracle within itself, which means we are a bunch of little miracles all wrapped up into one.

We are worthy of all things through hard work, dedication, integrity, and desire. There is nothing that can keep you from achieving your desires but you. If you want an ''A'' in your class, it's easy, just dedicate yourself to arriving to class on time, listening intently, taking notes, and exhibiting good study habits. If you do those things, you will receive the A you were seeking.

If you want to play a sport, the same applies—learn the sport, practice hard, and dedicate yourself to being the best athlete you can be. You have a much greater chance of succeeding as an athlete by following those rules.

If you want a promotion at your job, simply follow the same rules. Arrive on time; diligently study your position, which means learning your job; and go that extra mile to perfect your knowledge of the position. The supervisor will see your efforts and reward you with a promotion. We are all diamonds in the rough. Some are a little rougher than others, but we continue to be diamonds.

The same rules that apply in adolescent years apply in adulthood. If you develop good habits, there is nothing that you cannot conquer or achieve. Never doubt who you are. Remember, you are an *unlimited being*. You are a part of this world, and we need your contribution. Know what you are capable of. Do not underestimate yourself. *Know your worth.*

Your Turn

List your gifts

1._____

3._____

2._____

4._____

List your talents

1._____

3._____

2._____

4._____

List your skills

1._____

3._____

2._____

4._____

Entrepreneur tip:

Surround yourself with wise and influential individuals

Have a Mentor

*T**he world is vast, and there is an immense amount of information to be obtained.*** To help you along the way to becoming better prepared for success, you should have a mentor. A mentor is someone who is more experienced than his or her protégé. The mentor possesses the wisdom that is acquired through experience. The protégé is someone who wants to move up the ladder of success and utilizes the wisdom and experience of his or her mentor to accomplish that task. This mentor/protégé relationship should be a win-win for both parties. The protégé receives guidance and helpful advice from the mentor. The mentor benefits from the opportunity to enhance his or her leadership and communication skills.

When seeking out a mentor, choose someone who has goals similar to yours. Look for someone who is in the same career as you. Make sure you can devote the time that is required to learn from your mentor. You should seek out your mentor as you are the one who requires the help. Seek a mentor who also has the time required to mentor you.

If you examine successful individuals, you will find they typically had a mentor. They had someone they could confide in, who could enhance their knowledge. Most people underestimate the value of a mentor, but to be successful in business and entrepreneurship, you should have a mentor or coach, someone who is in the position that you are seeking. Mentors offer a wealth of knowledge and insight into things that only experience could bring to their protégés. Having a mentor will benefit you greatly. When you start to feel a little low, you will have someone to encourage and motivate you.

Valuable tips and information you obtain from your mentor will help to reduce the number of errors you make, alleviate your weaknesses, and allow you to build on your strengths. Your mentor has to be someone who will tell you the truth as situations occur. Honesty is a vital part of having a great mentor. It's great to know you have someone in your corner who will support you when you are developing your career. A mentor can:

- *Increase your self-confidence*
- *Develop your aspirations and optimism about the future*
- *Expand your insight*
- *Guide you through difficult situations*
- *Bring out the best in you*

Having a mentor is not required to become successful, but having a good mentor will shorten your trip to success and help you to stay in the game when things get tough. Bill Gates has Warren Buffet as a mentor. Warren Buffet is one of the wealthiest investors in the country. This association lends credence to the theory that you should find a mentor who is in the place in life that you are seeking. If you want to become number one in golf, then seek Tiger Woods for your mentor. To become a great talk show host, seek out Oprah Winfrey. To become a successful basketball player in the NBA, you should seek out Michael Jordan as a mentor.

If you don't have a mentor, seek one before you are in need of one. Choosing a mentor is a very important decision. You do not want to make that decision under any type of pressure. Start as early as middle and high school with peer counseling, a forum where you are able to obtain mentoring assistance and/or provide mentoring assistance amongst your peers. Also, a great way to pay it forward is by being a mentor to someone else.

My Mentors

I am fortunate to have had great mentors in my life. My mom and dad were my mentors. My mom and dad were entrepreneurs. My dad owned a very successful lawn service for over forty years.

He started his business from scratch with one lawn mower and one customer. I watched him impose no limitations on himself. He was not an educated man, but he was a hardworking man who believed that you give 150 percent to everything you do. He continuously learned as much as possible about his craft. I watched my dad take a lawn mower, one customer, and an unshakeable will to succeed and turn his business into a very successful company.

My mom was a homemaker with six kids and a dog. We were not rich, so my mom became a seamstress and made all of our clothes. She became so proficient in sewing that she began sewing for the neighbors. Eventually, my mother started to take on more and more customers. The extra money allowed our family to take vacations and live comfortably. My mom followed my dad's footsteps and directions to become an entrepreneur also.

I inherited my parent's entrepreneurial spirit. I worked a nine-to-five shift until I could pursue my entrepreneurial dream. I am now a mentor for several individuals and encourage them to pay it forward and become a mentor to someone else.

Write about your mentor or the mentor you would like to have.

_____

_____

_____

_____

_____

_____

_____

1. How have you benefited from having a mentor?

_____

_____

2. What skills have you developed or enhanced?

_____

_____

3. Do you have a career plan?

_____

_____

Pay It Forward
Pass It On
Share

It all means the same. Don't let the buck stop with you. Pass it on; pay it forward; share. Someone at some point helped you along the way. Who helped guide you in a certain direction? Be a blessing to someone else. Your blessing will not always be monetary, but you will always achieve inner satisfaction, which can do wonders for your mental, physical, and spiritual well-being.

"To whom much is given, much is expected." That phrase is so true. As you begin to create your empire, remember that phrase. Imagine yourself having a closed fist. That represents closing something in, protecting something within your hand. Hold it close and tightly. Nothing comes in between your fingers, and nothing comes out between your fingers. This is something you never want to experience. That closed fist represents a closed mind, a selfish nature, and an unmovable spirit. To begin to prosper, you will need to freely help those whom you determine you can help. I'm not implying you give away money; what I am saying is that you should share your wisdom, knowledge, and entrepreneurial spirit with the next person. Share my book; share other materials that will help others to the path to create their own empire.

"I would rather be the co-star of 99 autobiographies than be the star of one." —*Michael Baisden, radio and TV personality*

The quote from Michael Baisden means that it is better to assist ninety-nine individuals with their success, than to concentrate on yours alone. This is a prime example of paying it forward. The secret to wealth is helping others.

Part Four

Rich in
Thoughts

Journal Your Thoughts

Law and Order

There are rules that everyone must follow. Without rules to create order, there would be chaos. Implement order in your life and business, or you may find yourself in trouble with the law.

1. Live by your values.
2. Identify what is not working for you and get rid of it.
3. Follow the rules.

Any business owner will tell you that reputation is a vital ingredient in having a successful business. Treat your business like your life. Have integrity and honesty, and let your word be your bond. A good reputation will advance your life and business; a bad one can hinder your advancement.

Live by values, rules, and the law, and propel yourself forward.

Entrepreneur tip:

Always have order in your life.

Your turn

List some of your most important values

1.

2.

3.

4.

List some of the things you do that is not producing positive results

1.

2.

3.

4.

List the things you need to do that would produce positive results

_1._

_2._

_3._

_4._

Don't Climb the Mountain

*N*o matter what you want to do in life, you must learn and apply that knowledge. If one door closes, another door will open. There's an old saying that states:

"Give me the strength to climb that mountain and get to the other side where better things lie."
—Anonymous

The average Joe will gather up all his energy and begin climbing. A successful entrepreneur will figure out how to go through that mountain with the least amount of effort and maximum effectiveness. It is the same mountain, but these people use two different ways of getting to the other side. Become the mountain buster.

Journal Your Thoughts

Live Your Dream

Live your dream, and enjoy your life. Plan your life to enjoy your dreams. Most of us, thinking back as young as we can remember, have probably heard someone tell us at one time or another to get real and quit dreaming. That old expression of "Quit dreaming and come down to earth" might not be so unfamiliar to some of us. We're all dreamers in one form or another. As children, we thought nothing was impossible, and then we grew a little older and some folks, often the ones who loved us most, dampened our dreams and aspirations.

Live your dream, and enjoy your life. Life and the quality of life are important. Life is so precious because we never know what tomorrow will bring. Tomorrow holds no promise to anyone. But what we dream today stands as a foundation for many tomorrows.

Dreams bring about ideas which, in turn, are made into reality. The biggest dreamers in history made tremendous advances for other generations to enjoy: the Wright brothers and the airplane, Edison and the light bulb, Alexander Graham Bell and the telephone, Henry Ford and the automobile, and the biggest dreamer of them all Walt Disney with Disneyland and Disney World. They all had a dream. The seed was planted in their minds, and they did whatever it took to achieve that dream. They lived out their dreams. They allowed no distraction to stand in their way. Complacency is just a fancy word for laziness. Don't allow yourself to become lazy, and most of all, *never give up!*

Winston Churchill, one of Great Britain's greatest prime ministers, during that country's darkest time, gave a commencement speech to his old alma mater's graduating class. In what many historians today believe was one of his shortest speeches ever, he said,

> This is the lesson: never give in, never give in, never, never, never, never—in nothing, great or small, large or petty— never give in except to convictions of honor and good sense. Never yield to force; never yield to the apparently overwhelming might of the enemy.*

If you've been knocked down five times by that enemy, no matter who or what that might have been, make sure you rise again five times. The word *failure* goes hand in hand with success. We learn from our failures, but that word cannot be a part of your vocabulary. Failure is not an option. It may stand in your path to success. But success is your only option and ultimate end. Do not measure your success against or compare your success to the successes of others.

We are all individuals, and what lies within you is unique to only you and you alone. By the same token, do not envy the successes of others, for that will only dampen your own success. My definition of success and your definition of success could be worlds apart.

For some, having an empire may consist of having just enough money and assets to live a comfortable life with no financial worries or economic stress. For others, it may require fancier cars, a larger home or a second or third vacation home, a bigger yacht, or any one of many things they could not obtain before their empire was created. Whatever makes you happy and works well for you can make up your personal empire.

Always remember that you must sacrifice and be willing to do today the things that others are not willing to do, so tomorrow you can do what those others cannot.

---

*   **Harrow School, October 29, 1941 at Oxford or Cambridge.**

In the beginning of this chapter, I wrote, "Live your dream and enjoy your life." Plan your life so you can enjoy your dreams. A friend of mine once told me his definition of time. He asked me, "What is time? Time is life. Consequently, if you don't plan your time, you're not planning your life."

So, remember, no dream is too small and no dream is too big.

Live your dream and enjoy your life!

You are high school rich now!

*W*rite down a list of your dreams and see how they may have changed from the list you made at the beginning of the book.

1._____

_____

_____

_____

_____

2._____

_____

_____

_____

_____

3._____

_____

_____

_____

_____

Future

1._____

_____

_____

_____

_____

2._____

_____

_____

_____

3._____

_____

_____

_____

_____

Don't be afraid to *believe that you can have what you want and deserve*. Choose to be a champion; choose to be a champion chooser, and be willing to pay the price to fulfill all your goals and dreams. Be willing to be different. Fear not the unknown; fear the not knowing.

Kudos! You have taken the first step to creating your own empire. I wish you more success than you can imagine.

101 Hot Tips to Success

The following 101 hot tips to success are your recipe for success. Success is good judgment, self-discipline, perseverance, and all of the following. To get a better understanding of some of the tips below, choose five and write a paragraph on each of those you choose.

1. Dream big. No dream is too small and no dream is too big.

2. Prepare, prepare and prepare.

3. Be clear on what you want to achieve.

4. Know your strengths and build upon them.

5. Be realistic about your weaknesses. Identify and conquer it.

6. Have an open mind towards all endeavors.

7. Be goal-oriented to get ahead and achieve all your goals.

8. Be fully committed to every endeavor no matter how large or small.

9. Be motivated, stimulated and 100% interested in your endeavor.

10. Build on your strengths if you want to take your career to the next level.

11. Have clear expectations.

12. Be creative.

13. Prepare your finances.

14. Always be honest because honesty is the best policy.

15. Embrace criticism.

16. Be resilient.

17. Be a team builder.

18. Have discipline.

19. Use good communication skills.

20. Develop people skills.

21. Visualize success.

22. Surround yourself with successful people.

23. Continue to learn and educate yourself.

24. Quickly recover from failures.

25. Learn from your mistakes.

26. Be computer literate. Master your business software

27. Be a self-starter.

28. Stay focused.

29. Be conscientious.

30. Be hungry for success.

31. Use time management.

32. Look professional.

33. Act professional.

34. Think professional.

35. Dress professional.

36. Have enthusiasm.

37. Brainstorm.

38. Avoid negativity, it only drains your energy.

39. Be innovative.

40. Working hard equals success.

41. Be willing to learn.

42. Persevere.

43. Have balance in your business and personal life.

44. Discipline yourself.

45. Continuously network via social networking.

46. Think success.

47. Have a vision.

48. Utilize smart financing.

49. Create a solid foundation.

50. Look big even if your company is small.

51. Set realistic goals.

52. Develop a marketing strategy.

53. Choose your business carefully.

54. Make sure there is a demand for your business.

55. Develop a good reputation.

56. Find your niche.

57. Have determination.

58. Work smart.

59. Plan for success.

60. Value your customers. They are the meat of your business.

61. Seek constant improvement.

62. Be self-confident.

63. Have wise advisors.

64. Develop a recession-proof business that will withstand a failing economy.

65. Use listening skills to listen twice as much as you talk.

66. Be proficient with the Internet.

67. Be technology savvy.

68. Do what you love, and the money will follow.

69. Have a support system.

70. Write a business plan.

71. Know your tax responsibilities.

72. Develop a customer base that will help build referrals.

73. Have legal advisors that will give you good sound advice.

74. Start your business while still employed, until you can sustain yourself financially.

75. Have a positive attitude to draw positive actions.

76. Assess your talents.

77. Examine your skills and identify your strengths and weakness.

78. Protect your personal assets.

79. Get and keep a competitive edge.

80. Hire great people. Your company is as good as its weakest link.

81. Understand your business.

82. Pitch your ideas to someone smart.

83. Make sure you want to be a business owner.

84. Prepare for unsolicited advice. It could be helpful.

85. Master your marketing skills.

86. Specialize in what you love and the money will follow.

87. Surround yourself with positive people.

88. Build a team of competent employees.

89. Have professional advisors and continuously learn from them.

90. Get a mentor in your field of expertise.

91. Start small and watch your company grow and expand.

92. Watch expenses. Calculate your cost wisely.

93. Incorporate. Get the appropriate license via Sunbiz.org.

94. Have reliable suppliers whom you can trust to deliver as agreed.

95. Research the business.

96. Have all business agreements in writing.

97. Learn all about contracts.

98. Think rich. The power of thought can create success.

99. Use a catchy business name, easy to remember and pronounce.

100. Have organization skills.

101. Study your market/demographics. Know your customers.

The most successful men in the end are those whose success is the result of steady accretion...It is the man who carefully advances step by step, with his mind becoming wider and wider—and progressively better able to grasp any theme or situation—persevering in what he knows to be practical, and concentrating his thought upon it, who is bound to succeed in the greatest degree.

—Alexander Graham Bell

Choose Five Hot Tips to Discuss:

1._____

_____

_____

_____

_____

2._____

_____

_____

_____

_____

3._____

_____

_____

_____

_____

4._____

_____

_____

_____

_____

5._____

_____

_____

_____

_____

Part Five

Rich in Jobs

Journal Your Thoughts

Show Me the Money

Your high school years are formative. They are preparation for your upcoming college days and adulthood. Experts believe that part-time jobs increase a teen's sense of responsibility and ease the transition to the adult workplace. Follow a few basic rules when starting a job/business:

- Look for an industry that will truly engage you.
- Match the physical demands of your chosen business to your energy level.
- Understand the income potential and whether it matches your needs and how much you are comfortable investing.

As you earn money, remember to give back. The size of the donation is not what matters; all contributions help. Ten dollars donated to a mission could buy five meals for a family. Five dollars will buy ten notebooks at the local reading rooms. A donation of two dollars can provide a blanket to warm a person on a cold winter night. We all have a responsibility to assist our fellow man. Learn to share, pay it forward, and pass it on.

Dog Walking

*D*og *walking is more than just pulling an animal on a leash and getting some exercise.* You must have a genuine love for animals and concern for their well-being. Dogs need exercise to stay healthy and fit. Overweight dogs can have serious health conditions, which could shorten their life span and/or decrease the quality of their life. All dogs need to be walked, especially the ones that are inside all day.

Create your dog-walking business, and always remember, it is important to be an organized, professional, and dedicated person. If you are, you can have a rewarding dog-walking business.

Here are some suggestions on how to start your professional dog-walking business.

1. Consider how large you want your business to be. You may want to start small and allow time for growth. Trying to start a business too large and quickly can hinder your success.
2. Ask yourself how much time you can devote to your business. Be realistic in determining your hours of dedication. You cannot advertise a twenty-four-hour business and only have one hour a day to devote to the business.
3. Create some stylish business cards.
4. Make flyers and advertise in your neighborhood and community centers, and network with family and friends to get the word out about your business.

5. Research prices so you do not overcharge or undercharge your customers.

6. Create a good Web site. The Internet is becoming people's first port of call and aids them in the decision-making process. When choosing your domain name for your Web site, keep it simple, relevant, and targeted. Make sure the Web site is easy to access, has all of the necessary information about your services and fees for the dog-walking business, and last but not least, what appeals to your target audience. Do not gear your site toward people who won't need your services, like non-animal lovers or bird-watchers, just to name a few, if you want to build your business. Target your site toward animal lovers with the type of animal that requires walking.

Car Detailing

*C**ar detailing is a rewarding profession.* There are some things about car detailing that you must be knowledgeable of. Here's the list:

1. *Chemicals*, of course, refer to all the cleaning and protecting products that are used in detailing. The professional detailer should have on hand a set of products that, individually or combined, will handle virtually any vehicle surface problem. The professional detailer usually works with a local distributor, not only for the convenience of acquiring supplies, but also for getting quick answers to everyday detailing challenges.

2. *Equipment* is the tools of the trade. A lot of your information about these tools will come from your local detail supply shop, trade magazines, trade shows, equipment manufacturers, and other professionals in the industry. Take advantage of all these sources of information to build your knowledge of the tools required to do an outstanding job.

3. *Knowledge* of vehicle surfaces is essential in this business. You must understand how to rejuvenate and protect each of the many varied surfaces of a vehicle, regardless of the specific condition.

4. *Industry standards* are the standards that are set by the International Carwash Association (ICA). These standards are guidelines to follow to assist the professional detailer in rising to the top of the profession.

5. *Customer service* is one of the most important elements in the business. Ask your customer various questions before

the detailing process begins. When was the last time your car was detailed? What would you like to have done today? How much are you looking to spend today?

Babysitting

*B*abysitting *is a great job for preteens and teenagers.*
Many teens start out in this line of work by caring for younger siblings or helping out relatives with babies. You have connections with other parents and relatives, which can be a great resource in starting your business.

You must be mature and ready to handle any set of circumstances that might occur. A love for children is essential to having a great experience at all babysitting jobs. Here are some tips to get you started.

1. *Get your CPR and first-aid certification,* if you don't already have them. It is always better to be prepared for emergencies. Check with your local American Red Cross or hospital to see if they offer babysitting classes. The class is usually a daylong course, and sometimes there is a small fee to take the class and get your certification.
2. Decide how many *hours you can devote* to babysitting. Make sure to include time to rest and rejuvenate between each babysitting job. You have to be on alert and give your complete attention to the child you are babysitting.
3. Set rates based on the going rates in the area.
4. Create flyers and business cards. Utilize the Internet in a safe and secure manner.
5. Make sure to inform your parents of any and all clients you will babysit for. This is for safety reasons.

Lawn Service

*L*awn service is a business that will always exist as long as there is grass that grows. Lawn maintenance is a service business, and service businesses are the easiest, least expensive businesses to start. But don't be misled by the ease and low cost; they can also be *very profitable.* You can start your business with very little cash and build a very lucrative lawn-care business. You can make a great profit and only work part-time. Sounds like a profession that you should learn a little more about, don't you think? Here are a few tips:

1. Get a lawn mower, weed eater, and blower. This is the basic equipment that is required to start a lawn business.
2. Start with your neighborhood and inform you neighbors of your service. Knock on doors, distribute flyers and business cards, and use word of mouth.
3. Research prices to determine the fees that should be charged per home and service.
4. Learn as much as possible about lawns, trees, shrubs, lawn service contracts, and estimate forms. Take advantage of a free start-a-lawn-business course, which can be found on the Internet.
5. Calculate your start-up costs.
   Example: Used Lawn mower 30.00
             Used weed eater   15.00
             Used blower   10.00
             Service contracts   5.95
             _____
             $60.95   (approximate start-up costs)

Journal Your Thoughts

Other Businesses

Pressure Cleaning

Pressure cleaning means pressure-washing homes, driveways, and sidewalks. Some homes' water supply comes from wells. If left untreated, well water will leave rust stains on any areas that the water hits. Pressure cleaning is one of the fastest ways to remove these stains. Over time, the windows on high-rises and two- and three-story homes require washing. A pressure cleaner can reach these windows and strip the film of dirt away.

Hair Services_

Hair-care services include braiding, weaving, and haircuts. Your friends will all require a hair service at one time or another. It would be a great convenience to all if you could do it. Parents are extremely busy now, and your neighborhood service could be beneficial to both you and the customer. It seems it would be a win-win, for all involved. It could be the perfect way to start a business.

EBay Entrepreneur

EBay is an innovative way to sell various items. Instead of the old-school yard sale on the weekends, we now can sell every day of the week and not be concerned about the weather. EBay has phenomenal statistics on their selling.

Videographer

Many people need a videographer to help with their photos from the pre-Internet days. For many years, pictures were taken and stored in a shoe box or some other place in the home or office to be viewed at a later time—these include photos from birthday parties, social events, family gatherings, and of the elderly and others.

Appendix: Journal

Journal
Your
Thoughts

Entrepreneur tip:

When journaling, be complete, consistant and organized.

Enjoy journaling in the month

of

_____

Day 1

I am a champion.

Day 2

I choose to be successful.

Day 3

_____

_____

_____

_____

_____

_____

_____

_____

_____

_____

_____

_____

_____

_____

Visualize it, and achieve it.

Day 4

_____

_____

_____

_____

_____

_____

_____

_____

_____

_____

_____

_____

_____

_____

_____

Success starts in the mind.

Day 5

_____

_____

_____

_____

_____

_____

_____

_____

_____

_____

_____

_____

_____

_____

_____

Knowledge is power.

Day 6

Open your mind to prosperity.

Day 7

You are an unlimited being.

Day 8

Positive thinking is contagious.

Day 9

_____

_____

_____

_____

_____

_____

_____

_____

_____

_____

_____

_____

_____

_____

_____

Happy thoughts make your life happy.

Day 10

Success is manifested in small daily events.

Day 11

What you do today will affect your tomorrow.

Day 12

Positive thoughts equal positive results.

Day 13

Read, learn, and execute.

Day 14

Positive thoughts work together with positive actions.

Day 15

_____

_____

_____

_____

_____

_____

_____

_____

_____

_____

_____

_____

_____

_____

_____

_____

_____

Discipline, patience, and perseverance lead to success.

Day 16

Shrug off the setbacks
and courageously push forward.

Day 17

_____

_____

_____

_____

_____

_____

_____

_____

_____

_____

_____

_____

_____

_____

_____

_____

Always stand for integrity and honesty.

Day 18

Develop good time management.

Day 19

Brainstorm, brainstorm, brainstorm.

Day 20

Use the power of your imagination to create.

Day 21

Pay it forward.

Day 22

Read, absorb, and apply.

Day 23

_____

_____

_____

_____

_____

_____

_____

_____

_____

_____

_____

_____

_____

_____

_____

You are an unlimited being.

Day 24

Pay it forward.

Day 25

_____

_____

_____

_____

_____

_____

_____

_____

_____

_____

_____

_____

_____

_____

_____

_____

What is unique about you?

Day 26

Live, love, and laugh every day.

Day 27

Your mind has limitless potential.

Day 28

Think success, and you will have success.

Day 29

Have good health and a good mind and have great success.

Day 30

_____

_____

_____

_____

_____

_____

_____

_____

_____

_____

_____

_____

_____

_____

_____

_____

Value your friends.

Day 31

Life is what you make it.

Enjoy journaling in the month

of

_____

Day 1

I am a champion.

Day 2

I choose to be successful.

Day 3

Visualize it, and achieve it.

Day 4

Success starts in the mind.

Day 5

Knowledge is power.

Day 6

Open your mind to prosperity.

Day 7

You are an unlimited being.

Day 8

_____

_____

_____

_____

_____

_____

_____

_____

_____

_____

_____

_____

_____

_____

Positive thinking is contagious.

Day 9

Happy thoughts make your life happy.

Day 10

_____

_____

_____

_____

_____

_____

_____

_____

_____

_____

_____

_____

_____

_____

_____

_____

Success is manifested in small daily events.

Day 11

_____

_____

_____

_____

_____

_____

_____

_____

_____

_____

_____

_____

_____

_____

_____

_____

What you do today will affect your tomorrow.

Day 12

Positive thoughts equal positive results.

Day 13

Read, learn, and execute.

Day 14

Positive thoughts work together with positive actions.

Day 15

Discipline, patience, and perseverance lead to success.

Day 16

*Shrug off the setbacks
and courageously push forward.*

Day 17

_____

_____

_____

_____

_____

_____

_____

_____

_____

_____

_____

_____

_____

_____

_____

_____

Always stand for integrity and honesty.

Day 18

_____

_____

_____

_____

_____

_____

_____

_____

_____

_____

_____

_____

_____

_____

Develop good time management.

Day 19

Brainstorm, brainstorm, brainstorm.

Day 20

Use the power of your imagination to create.

Day 21

Pay it forward.

Day 22

Read, absorb, and apply.

Day 23

You are an unlimited being.

Day 24

Pay it forward.

Day 25

_____

_____

_____

_____

_____

_____

_____

_____

_____

_____

_____

_____

_____

_____

_____

What is unique about you?

Day 26

_____

_____

_____

_____

_____

_____

_____

_____

_____

_____

_____

_____

_____

_____

Live, love, and laugh every day.

Day 27

Your mind has limitless potential.

Day 28

Think success, and you will have success.

Day 29

Have good health and a good mind and have great success.

Day 30

_____

_____

_____

_____

_____

_____

_____

_____

_____

_____

_____

_____

_____

_____

Value your friends.

Day 31

_____

_____

_____

_____

_____

_____

_____

_____

_____

_____

_____

_____

_____

_____

_____

Life is what you make it

To contact the author

Wendy Perkins
P.O. Box 550811
Davie, Florida 33325
1-855-700-RICH

Internet address: www.highschoolrich.com

Suggested reading list

Inside The Dream: The personal story of Walt Disney
Hard Drive: Bill Gates, the Making of Microsoft
Grinding It Out: The Making of McDonald's

Coming in the future

Kindergarten Rich
Elementary Rich
Middle School Rich

Made in the USA
Charleston, SC
22 August 2011